PREACHING FROM

ISAIAH

by

JOHN P. MILTON

Augsburg Publishing House • Minneapolis

PREACHING FROM ISAIAH

Copyright 1953
Augsburg Publishing House

FOREWORD

The writing of this book is the result of a challenge and a conviction.

The challenge came from a young Lutheran pastor. Why, said he, could there not be an Old Testament lesson to be read at the morning worship in addition to the Epistle and the Gospel? Why should not an Old Testament series of texts be included in Lutheran hymnals for use in worship and preaching? My answer was that the suggestion seemed good to me; for the Old Testament is also a part of the Bible which we confess to be the Word of God and there is in it a religious message relevant for today, and yet this treasure remains largely unfamiliar to our people through lack of use. In my enthusiasm (for I love the Old Testament) I said to him: "You could find appropriate lessons for a complete Old Testament pericope series for the church year in the book of Isaiah alone!" His reply was a challenge: "Why not do it?"

The conviction concerns the value in observing the sequence of the church year in preaching and worship. The faithful observance of the church year has been the source of rich spiritual blessings to the Christian congregation. The preacher may sometimes feel that it cramps his style and interferes with his liberty, but it safeguards the right of the people to have the whole counsel of God preached to them. There is about it a simplicity of outline and a natural sequence of parts and a wide scope of Scriptural content that cannot fail to impress itself upon the faithful church member who participates regularly in the worship life of his church. If faithfully followed it makes for a well-balanced emphasis in preaching and for a well-rounded knowledge of Scripture on the part of the people who listen to the preaching.

It would be profitable to use the book of Isaiah for preaching for a year without concerning ourselves about a pericope system. It would be possible to go through the book chapter by chapter and by means of expository preaching to acquaint our people with the message of Isaiah. There is something to be said for such a procedure, especially if it can be done at the Sunday evening service. But my personal conviction is that the Lutheran Church would make a mistake if it sacrificed the treasure that it has in its lessons that follow the sequence of the church year, even if it did so in favor of a systematic study of significant Bible books. Because of this conviction I am bold to suggest that we try to use texts from Isaiah to enrich the church year instead of to take its place. It is my hope and belief that the lessons selected from Isaiah will help in preaching on the New Testament even when they are not used as sermon texts in their own right. It is my prayer that when they are used for preaching they will be seen always to unite with the message of the New Testament as one Word of God.

There is one explanation that needs to be made. This is not a commentary, nor is it a collection of sermon outlines. It has one humble purpose only: to help the reader (the preacher) to see some of the religiously relevant teachings of the text and to relate them to the central theme in other lessons for the same day. This book is not a substitute for personal effort in sermon preparation. It may give some help and inspiration to the preacher who wishes above all else to be a Biblical preacher but who feels that there is room for growth in his own Bible knowledge as well as in that of his people. In a special sense the book is dedicated to the students at Luther Theological Seminary who have made my teaching of the book of Isaiah a joyous privilege.

Grateful acknowledgment is made to Augustana Book Concern for permission to use many of the topical headings from the lectionary in the Augustana hymnal. The author is indebted to Bo Giertz for helpful hints from his analysis of the church year in his book for confirmands, "Grunden."

The scripture quotations in the book are from the REVISED STANDARD VERSION of the Bible, copyrighted 1946 and 1952 by the Division of Christian Education, National Council of Churches, and used by permission.

THE AUTHOR.

The Historical Milieu
of the Book of Isaiah

In preaching from Isaiah or from any of the prophets it is important to know something of the historical setting of the message.

If we were to characterize the prophets and their ministry three things (at least) must be said about them. They were first of all men of vision, men who possessed a unique spiritual insight and were able to speak with spiritual authority. They were also men with a message for their own day and age, men who preached the word of God and applied it to the contemporary situation. Finally, they were men with a living hope, men who interpreted not only the present but the future in the light of God's covenant and predicted events that would lead to the ultimate goal of the covenant of blessing with Abraham which in Christ includes the world.

It is obvious that if the prophetic message had relevancy for the historical situation to which it was first addressed a knowledge of that historical situation will help us to understand the message. What did the message mean in the way of judgment threat or of redemptive hope to the people of the prophet's own day? Preaching—if it be good preaching—necessarily reflects in both form and content something of the present situation which gives occasion for it: it is directed to its need; it is colored by its experiences; it is expressed in its language. It is in a good sense of the word contemporaneous.

That does not imply that it is necessarily limited to the immediate historical milieu. For the prophetic message is often also eschatological; it sees the present as a junction between the past and the future; it is conscious always of God's eternal covenant purpose and of the significance of the present experience or event in relation to that purpose; and it frequently looks forward to what is called in Acts 3:21 (ASV), "the times of restoration of all things," the ultimate Divine goal, whether we look at it from the viewpoint of His covenant, or of His redemption, or of His revelation. But here too it is important to know the immediate historical background for the prophecy; for even in eschatological preaching, which includes the element of prediction, prophecy has this unique feature of uniting in one blended picture the final goal and intermediate steps that lead up to it. The "times-coloring" of the prophecy (to borrow Ed. Riehm's expressive phrase) is that of an event within the historical horizon of the prophet and of his people, and the prophecy may indeed find a partial fulfilment in that event; but there are in the prophetic message spiritual depths and sometimes specific predictions that point beyond it to the ultimate goal of God's covenant.

Obviously, it is well to know the history insofar as it helps us to see through the "times-coloring" to the eternal spiritual principles involved and to the ultimate goal of God's redemptive activity indicated under the covenant. The very covenant with Abraham and with his seed, especially in the form which it took with Israel as a nation, provides significant historical "times-coloring" for the prophetic preaching—if indeed we admit that when they speak of Israel's or of Zion's happy future as a redeemed people the prophecy may have ultimate reference to the Christian dispensation. In the latter part of the book of Isaiah it is the redemption from Babylon that provides "times-coloring" for a message of redemption that in its essential features points to the eternal redemption of Christ. Historically the one redemption-experience foreshadows and prepares the way for the other. Spiritually they involve the same fundamental spiritual principles expressed in similar promises. In the prophetic preaching they seem sometimes to be joined as one, even as the mountain ranges of the west when seen from a distance are one; it was not always given to the prophets to see clearly "the times and the seasons" (see I Peter 1:10, 11). But if we understand the relationship between the two it is perfectly legitimate to take a text that speaks in the first instance of the return from captivity in Babylon and to preach on the theme of God's redemption as a "continuing theological principle" which is finally fulfilled in the eternal redemption through the blood of Jesus Christ. There may be more than one phase to the fulfilment of a prophecy, wherefore it is correct to speak at times of "its highest fulfilment" in Christ. The "times-coloring" belongs to the local situation, but it has vital significance in helping us to understand eternal truths. The life and ministry of Isaiah belongs to the latter half of the 8th century B. C.

There are several significant notices in the book that help to place him in relation to the history of Judah (and of Israel, the northern kingdom, as well). The first of these in order of importance is in ch. 6, where his call and commissioning as a prophet is said to have taken place in the year that King Uzziah died. That would be approximately 740 B. C., or perhaps slightly later (734 B. C., Westminster Bible Dictionary). According to G. A. Smith it is more than a date; there is a great contrast suggested between "the king, Uzziah" (vs. 1) and "the king, Jehovah of hosts" (vs. 5), or between the eclipsed glory of Uzziah and the earth-filling glory of the Lord. It was a "crisis" year in the history of God's people. We can see that crisis in the transition from Uzziah, a relatively good king (II Kings 15:3), to Ahaz, who was of a different spirit (II Kings 16:2-4). If the chronology in the Westminster Historical Atlas to the Bible is correct and Jotham's reign was that of a co-regent preceding Uzziah's death, during his years of retirement as a leper, the transition was a sharp one, spiritually as well as politically. We can see the crisis also in the end of a long and prosperous reign, an era of God's favor, which nevertheless left the people unaffected at heart by God's goodness as well as by His chastisement. And the crisis can be seen most sharply in the changed foreign policy inaugurated by Ahaz, because of his unbelief (see Isaiah 7; II Kings 16:10 ff.), which brought Judah for the first time directly within the sphere of influence of the great Gentile world empires. There is from here on a steady decline in Judah's position of independence as a nation; it is in a sense the beginning of the times of the Gentiles (Luke 21:24). In that crisis God needed a prophet to speak for Him, to interpret the present and to predict the future in the light of the covenant purpose from the past.

The statement in ch. 1:1 indicates something of the length and duration of Isaiah's ministry. Beginning in the last year of King Uzziah, it continued on through the reign of Ahaz into that of Hezekiah who reigned from 725 B. C. to 697 B. C. (Westminster Historical Atlas). The Sennacherib invasion took place in 701 B. C.; hence it is safe to say that the prophetic ministry of Isaiah covered a period of at least 40 years, from approximately 740 B. C. to the end of the century. It has been conjectured that he lived on into the reign of the wicked Manasseh in the first part of the 7th century (see the reference to the death of Sennacherib and the accession of Esarhaddon, 681 B. C., in Isaiah 37: 38). If Isaiah was a young man of 20 at the time of his call he could have lived twenty years beyond the turn of the century and still have been only 80 years old when he died.

It is important to note also the historical references in the book of Isaiah to foreign powers such as Assyria and Babylon. The ministry of Isaiah lies within what is commonly called the Assyrian period in political world history. In 745 B. C., after Assyrian power had been in a slight decline for some time, Tiglath-pileser III came to the throne and soon began to push Assyrian conquests westward and southward. This is the Assyrian ruler who is called Pul in II Kings 15:19 and is referred to by his true name of Tiglath-pileser in II Kings 15:29 (see also II Kings 16:7,10). The Assyrian aggression is reflected in many ways in the book of Isaiah, especially in chapters 1—12. Though we cannot date each chapter and verse in exact terms of the Assyrian schedule of conquest a knowledge of the general situation sheds helpful light in the study of the prophecy. It is well to keep in mind such dates as the accession of Tiglath-pileser to the throne in 745, the fall of Damascus in 732, the fall of Samaria in 722, and the Sennacherib invasion of Judah in 701 which failed to achieve the fall of Jerusalem. Sennacherib's invasion and his siege of Jerusalem is presented in religious-historical form in chs. 36—37. There seems to be an Assyrian background also for much of the material in chs. 28—33.

In the latter part of the book the political world situation as well as the national situation of Judah is different. Judah is a people in captivity and in need of redemption. Especially in chapters 40—48 it is evident that the reference is to the Babylonian Captivity. What is commonly called the Babylonian situation began to develop a century later than the call of Isaiah to prophetic service. During the Assyrian period political power and dominion was concentrated at Nineveh, with Babylon in the role of a vassal city. In 626 B. C., however, Babylon regained its independence, and with the overthrow of Nineveh in 612 B. C., the Chaldean (Babylonian) empire supplanted the Assyrian. In 606-605 B. C., after the battle of Carchemish and the defeat of Pharaoh Necho of Egypt, the might of the new world power was first directed against Judah, and in 586 B. C. Jerusalem was captured and destroyed by Nebuchadnezzar and the people carried into a captivity which did not end until the Medo-Persians took over from the Chaldeans and Cyrus issued his decree in 538 that permitted the Jews to return to their homeland. The Babylonian Captivity belongs therefore in the main to the 6th Century B. C. The message in chs. 40—48 is clearly directed to a people in exile; it is a message of their imminent redemption, a message of comfort and hope in both a national and a spiritual sense. Though there is no direct reference to Babylon after ch. 48 the "captivity" background can be seen in many places even in these later chapters. It is this fact which confronts us so sharply with the question of authorship for chs. 40—66. If they are from the Isaiah of the 8th century they are pure prediction, with a message of redemption to a people not yet in captivity and therefore not yet in need of the message. If, as so many Bible students now believe, they are from another (anonymous) prophet who lived in the 6th century, they are the proclamation of comfort, redemption, and release to a people in captivity whose purpose is to create new faith and hope in the covenant faithfulness of God and at the same time to shed new light on both the nature and the goal of God's redemption. There is something to be said on both sides of this question of authorship. It is not necessary to decide the question here; but it is important that in our preaching we recognize the Babylonian background for the message. That is definitely a part of the "times-coloring" which belongs to the prophecy; but certainly the prophecy is not limited to the return from Babylon, even if we rightly stress the spiritual aspect of that deliverance as well as the political. "The clothes are too big," the language is too exalted, the outlook is too far-reaching, to fit the redemption from Babylon alone; the conception that underlies the prophecy is that of the ultimate and complete fulfilment of what God has purposed for His people under His ancient covenant with them: and the very return from the captivity revealed its insufficiency to measure up to the grandeur and glory visualized in the prophecy. The prophecy points forward through the "times-coloring" to the time of the end, or to "the latter days," to the consummation of God's covenant in Christ and in His Church, even to the day when He shall make all things new in the new heavens and the new earth which He will create. It is not always easy to preach from the prophets and to play fair with both the historical and the eschatological aspects of their message; but let not that which is difficult dissuade us from the attempt! If we emphasize the continuing theological principles such as the judgment and the redemption motifs that run through the Old Testament and the New Testament alike, we shall not go far astray in our preaching. God is always engaged in judgment, but He is moving on towards a final judgment. God is always engaged in redemption, but He moves on towards the final redemption. The steps along the way point forward to the final goal. The goal is in Christ, not for one nation only but for the world, a redemption not only from sin but from death, a complete restoration to the bliss that was lost in the fall. The glory of the book of Isaiah is like that of the book of Revelation; it starts in the mundane present and then proceeds to encompass heaven and earth; but always its main theme is that of the covenant of blessing with Abraham, the promise of God to dwell with His people as their God, Redeemer, Saviour, and King. That promise was true in the 8th century B. C., in the return from the Babylonian Captivity, in the life and ministry of our Lord Jesus Christ. It is true now in the Church, and according to a faithful prophecy, it shall be gloriously true eternally in the new heavens and the new earth which God will make.

First Sunday in Advent

TOPIC FOR THE DAY: "The Coming of the Lord to His Church."

TEXT: Isaiah 62:10-12.

THEME: Behold, your salvation comes!

Relation of the text to the topic:

The text is tied up with the general thought and theme for the day through the statement, "Behold, your salvation comes." The parallelism of the verse shows that "your salvation" is here equivalent to "your Saviour." The Saviour from whom this salvation comes is the LORD. The nature of the salvation is still seen in terms of the covenant with Israel. There is to be a return from captivity, vs. 10. There is to be a realization at last of Israel's calling to be a holy people, vs. 12; see Exodus 19:6. They are to become in a renewed sense the redeemed of the LORD and to experience His abiding presence and fellowship, vs. 12; see Exodus 19:5-6.

The fulfilment of such a prophecy has universal spiritual implications. If the covenant of blessing with Abraham aimed at the day when "all nations" should be blessed in his seed (see Galatians 3:14), then this prophecy too must find its real fulfilment in Christ and in His Church. We need not hesitate to apply it in this spiritual New Testament sense, though in so doing we should not lose sight of its original reference to Israel as the Old Testament people of God. There is an historical continuity and a spiritual unity to be seen in Scripture between the Old Testament Israel and the New Testament Church, with the point of union in Christ through whom by faith we also are Abraham's offspring and heirs according to promise; see Gal. 3:29. The Augustana lectionary rightly includes this text from Isaiah as one of the lessons for the First Sunday in Advent.

Basic religious teachings of the text:

1. The coming of salvation as an act of God. 2. The threefold results of this salvation: (a) Consecration, or sanctification. "The holy people"; (b) Deliverance: "The redeemed of the LORD"; (c) Divine fellowship: "Sought out, a city not forsaken."

New Testament echoes of the text:

1. In Matthew 21:5, where a line from Isaiah 62:11 seems to be combined with a quotation from Zechariah 9:9.

2. The concept of a holy people is reflected in I Peter 2:9; see also I Peter 1:13-16. Both Isaiah and Peter speak against the background of Exodus 19:6.

3. The concept of redemption is taken up in the New Testament and is given there its full spiritual and eternal content. Isaiah 62:11 is very similar to Isaiah 40:10; see also Isaiah 35:9. The "forward look" of these prophetic passages is to a final redemption wherein God's covenant with Abraham and with Israel, with all its spiritual implications, should be fully and finally realized. It required the New Testament to make it clear that this "eternal redemption" has been secured for us by Jesus Christ, and to give us final insight into the deep spiritual nature of that redemption.

Second Sunday in Advent

TOPIC FOR THE DAY: "Waiting for the Day of the Lord."

TEXT: Isaiah 11:1-10.

THEME: The righteous reign of the root of Jesse (or the Messiah).

Relation of the text to the topic:

The theme of the texts for this day is the Second Coming of Christ, or his return in glory to judge the earth and to establish his kingdom with victory. The New Testament refers to this coming event as "the time for establishing all that God spoke by the mouth of His holy prophets from of old" (Acts 3:21). The Old Testament looks forward to such a time of consummation and pictures it as the fulfilment of the covenant and as the goal of the Messianic hope under the covenant. However, according to the "shortened perspective" of prophecy, near and distant events are often blended in one picture, with no attempt to determine the time-relationship between them. Such is the prophecy in Isaiah 11. It begins with a prediction of the Messiah's lowly origin, as we see him at his first Advent, vs. 1. It continues with a description of his spiritual endowment, vs. 2. It goes on to describe this Spirit-led, Spirit-endowed ruler in action, vs. 3-5. Much of the picture applies to Christ's spiritual reign now in the Church; for that reign is indeed characterized by righteousness and faithfulness. But there is in vs. 4 a hint of a greater and final judgment upon the earth which is still future; and in vs. 6-9 we see the prophetic hope and promise of what the earth shall be like after this judgment. The marks of that new age which is God's goal for human history are a state of peace like that in Paradise before the fall, and a knowledge of God that fills the earth. For such a day we wait and watch and work and pray. The evangelization of the Gentiles, vs. 10, and the restoration of Israel, vs. 11-16, are related to that day, perhaps as events which help to prepare the way.

Basic religious teachings of the text:

1. Concerning the Messiah: a) His humble origin; b) His spiritual endowment, with wisdom, might, and the fear of the Lord; c) His spiritual activity now, which is in righteousness and faithfulness; d) His future judgment on the wicked.

2. The goal of God's redemptive activity in history, which the Messiah will usher in: righteousness and peace, and a knowledge of God which leads to right action.

New Testament echoes of the text:

1. His humble origin is reflected in the nativity story and in Philippians 2:5-8.

2. The resting of the Spirit upon him is reflected in the narrative of his baptism, Matthew 3:16, and in the statement in Acts 10:38, "God anointed Jesus of Nazareth with the Holy Spirit and with power."

3. The slaying of the wicked "with the breath of his lips" reminds of the statement in II Thessalonians 2:8 that the Lord Jesus shall slay the lawless one "with the breath of his mouth." Both prophecies look forward to events yet to come.

4. In the New Testament Jesus is called "the Holy and Righteous One," Acts 3:14. He preached much about righteousness. See Matthew 5-7. His life and death manifested a righteousness of God which can be ours by faith in Christ. See Romans 3-4. His final judgment is a righteous judgment, II Thessalonians 1:5-6.

5. The Old Testament concept of "that day" as a day when God would bring to completion that which He has shown to be the purpose of His covenant is carried over into the New Testament anticipation and hope of the return of Christ in glory.

Third Sunday in Advent

TOPIC FOR THE DAY: "The Forerunner of the Lord."

TEXT: Isaiah 40:1-8.

THEME: Prepare the way of the Lord!

Relation of the text to the topic:

On this Sunday in Advent the emphasis is on the man who was sent as a messenger before the face of Jesus to prepare the way for him. That man was John the Baptist. Isaiah speaks of him prophetically as "the voice of one crying in the wilderness," and Malachi calls him, in behalf of God, "my messenger." Both prophets speak of his work as that of preparing the way for the Lord to come to His people. The Lord had a message of comfort for His people. We can see a reference in this word of consolation to the return of Israel from the Babylonian Captivity. We can also see a reference to a renewal of God's covenant with His people to be their God and to restore the fellowship with Himself which had been broken by their sin. In a deeper sense we can see that both covenant and prophetic word point forward to a fulfilment in Christ who was to be "Immanuel," "God with us," and through whom all men, and every sinner, should hear the good news of the gospel. The preparation for such a preaching of the gospel in any age is first to preach repentance. That levels the road for God to come as the Saviour into the hearts of sinners with a message of comfort. Such a preaching of repentance was the mission of John, and of many others before and after him. The text can be applied to every true minister, who is also called to preach repentance and thus prepare the way for the Saviour. However, to John came the distinct honor of being the immediate historical forerunner and herald of the King and by his preaching to prepare the way for Jesus. Where men are brought to repentance by such preaching the gospel has a chance to come with its message of comfort, so that "by the encouragement of the scriptures we might have hope," Romans 15:4. This word of our God shall stand forever.

Basic religious teachings of the text:
1. God's willingness to comfort His people with salvation and with forgiveness when they have sinned.
2. The need of preparing the way for the comfort of the gospel by the preaching of true repentance.
3. The abiding truth of God's Word for a humanity that is like withering grass.

New Testament echoes of the text:
1. It is the interpretation of Isaiah 40:3-5 in Luke 3:3-6 and in Matthew 3:1-3 that enables us to see its ultimate fulfilment in the ministry of John when he preached the baptism of repentance unto the remission of sins.
2. The comfort of which Paul speaks in II Corinthians 1:3-7 is more than superficially related to the comfort which God commanded through Isaiah to be preached to Jerusalem in a definite historical situation; and both are definitely related to the gospel as good news for the sinner who is afflicted for his sins.

Fourth Sunday in Advent

TOPIC FOR THE DAY: "The Lord Is at Hand."
TEXT: Isaiah 51:1-8.
THEME: My salvation is near!

Relation of the text to the topic:
It is natural that the last Sunday in Advent should emphasize the nearness of the Lord's coming, and the joy that the thought inspires.

We see both of these emphases in the lessons for the day. In some it is the joy of anticipation on the part of John in his witness of Jesus at his first Advent. It was his happy privilege to announce to his own generation that the Saviour already stood in their midst. The Lord was at hand! In others there is the joyous thought that the Lord is ever near with His salvation when we look unto Him in prayer. In one, the epistle lesson from Philippians 4, the comforting sentence that "the Lord is at hand" may refer to the hope of Jesus' return in glory.

The same truth of the nearness of God and of His salvation is stressed in the lesson from Isaiah 51. Encouraged by the remembrance of God's covenant with Abraham in the past, he proclaims the comfort and the joy of God's salvation in the present distress of His people, and then looks to the future with the declaration that God's righteous salvation not only is near but shall be forever. The salvation of God is always near to them that call upon Him in truth. There was an experience of salvation in the Old Testament, even in the return of the covenant people from captivity; yet, historically, the prophet's words apply in the full sense to the salvation that Jesus Christ came to bring. This Advent Sunday reminds us that in him God's promise and prediction is fulfilled: "My deliverance draws near speedily, my salvation has gone forth —my deliverance will be forever, and my salvation to all generations."

Basic religious teachings of the text:

1. The importance of remembering what God has said and done in the past as an encouragement to faith in the present.

2. The spiritual significance of the covenant of blessing with Abraham in relation to the history of Israel and the coming of salvation through Jesus Christ.

3. "My deliverance" (ASV "my righteousness") and "my salvation," thrice repeated, express the attitude of God and His redemptive activity in relation to His people always; but they are fully expressed in Jesus Christ.

4. The truth of the nearness and of the joy of salvation.

New Testament echoes of the text:

1. With respect to the ultimate purpose and goal of God's covenant of blessing with Abraham, see Galatians 3:8, 13-14.

2. With respect to the salvation of God as Isaiah speaks of it, see the Magnificat (Luke 1:46-55), the Benedictus (Luke 1:67-79), the Nunc Dimittis (Luke 2:28-32), and the quotation from Isaiah 40 in Luke 3:3-6. What the Old Testament says in somewhat general terms about the salvation of God is in the New Testament applied specifically to salvation in Christ.

Christmas Day

TOPIC FOR THE DAY: "The Nativity."

TEXT: Isaiah 9:1-7.

THEME: For to us a child is born, to us a son is given!

Relation of the text to the topic:

Any Old Testament prophecy which is a direct prediction of the coming of the Messiah is an appropriate text for Christmas Day. There are several such prophecies in the book of Isaiah. This prophecy, however, is the one that fits the occasion best because it speaks so directly of the birth of the Messiah and at the same time so fully of the nature and the results of his ministry. The New Testament identifies it as a Messianic prediction which found at least a partial fulfilment in the Galilean ministry of Jesus.

The immediate historical background for the prophecy is the beginning of the Assyrian invasion and conquest. According to II Kings 15: 29 Tiglath-pileser of Assyria took "Gilead, and Galilee, all the land of Naphtali" and carried them captive to his own land. It marked the beginning of a judgment darkness upon God's covenant people, which seemed to threaten the very existence of the covenant with Abraham and with Israel, and to frustrate the fulfilment of God's purpose with that covenant. The prophecy makes it clear that God is not defeated in His purpose by temporary setbacks. The faithful God will not let Himself be thwarted by an unfaithful people. The blended perspective of prophecy helps us to understand the picture given by the prophet. It is a picture which unites earthly and spiritual elements, and which combines near and remote events, in order to focus the eye of faith and hope on a coming Davidic king of grand proportions, who will at last establish God's kingdom of righteousness and peace among men. Only a complete sermon could illustrate adequately how this rich Old Testament text can be applied to Jesus Christ of whom it so clearly speaks.

Basic religious teachings of the text:

We could take any verse of this prophecy and find in it a glorious Christmas message; for every verse is linked with the key-verse and its announcement, "For to us a child is born, to us a son is given," and this child we believe on the basis of Scripture and of history to be the holy Child of Bethlehem.

1. We could think of him as the light of the world (vs. 2), the everlasting light that shone in the darkness that enveloped the little town of Bethlehem, and has been shining out into the spiritual darkness of the world ever since.

2. We could think of him as the Prince of Peace (vs. 6), and pause to inquire what kind of peace he has to offer, and whether there is reality to be looked for in the angelic announcement to the shepherds, "Peace on earth."

3. We could think of him in connection with the joy that is promised (vs. 3), remembering what Jesus said, "These things I speak in the world, that they may have my joy fulfilled in themselves" (John 17:13).

4. We could speak of deliverance from a bondage like unto that in the day of Midian (vs. 4) and make no mistake in connecting it with the deliverance "from all manner of evil, whether it affect the body or the soul" for which Jesus taught us to pray in the seventh petition of the Lord's Prayer.

5. We could think of him as the King, whose government is upon his shoulder (vs. 7); the true son of David, whose kingdom (according to his own confession) is not of this world (John 18:36, 37); and yet, the day shall come when "the kingdom of the world has become the kingdom of our Lord and of his Christ, and he shall reign for ever and ever" (Rev. 11:15).

6. And we could run through the list of names given him (vs. 6), and see the peculiar fitness of each when applied to Jesus Christ, from the designation "Wonderful Counselor" to the name that stands in cli-

mactic position and sums up all that which this child should represent in relation to human life, "Prince of Peace."

This is a rich prophetic word that tells of glory for them who have suffered contempt, of light for darkness, of joy in place of sorrow, of deliverance for the oppressed, of a day when peace shall take the place of war: all because a child is born, who is the gift of God's love to men, and who comes to subdue man's rooted enmity, and to subject all things under his feet, in a reign of righteousness and of peace. Even after making due allowance for the local "times-coloring" of the Assyrian situation the spiritual principles involved which found their fulfilment in Christ are evident.

New Testament echoes of the text:

1. The clearest reference is in Matthew 4:12-16, where the claim is made that Isaiah 9:1-2 was fulfilled in Jesus' Galilean ministry. In view of the structural unity of the passage in Isaiah it is clear that the effect of the interpretation is to connect the whole prophecy with Christ.

2. The concepts of light, joy, deliverance, righteousness, and peace are all familiar New Testament concepts.

3. The names of the child (vs. 6) are all closely related to still clearer New Testament assertions concerning Christ.

4. The language of verse 7 closely resembles the words of the angel Gabriel in the Annunciation to the Virgin Mary (Luke 1:32, 33). The emphasis is on a Davidic king, with an eternal kingdom (Rev. 11:15) of righteousness and peace, the twin goals of all prophecy.

Second Day of Christmas

Topic for the Day: "The Martyrs."

Text: Isaiah 26:16-21

Theme: Come, my people—hide yourselves for a little while until the wrath is past.

Relation of the text to the topic:

This is the day of St. Stephen, the first Christian martyr. It is interesting to note that it stands in such close proximity to the day of the

Nativity of him whom the martyrs confessed as Son of God and Saviour, and sealed that confession with their blood. It is unfortunate that it is now seldom celebrated in our churches; for the theme of the Second Day of Christmas is not primarily the sufferings of the martyrs, but rather their confession of their faith even unto death.

It is the suffering and persecution element in Isaiah 26:16-21, however, that unites it with the other texts for the day. The prophet speaks of a time of trouble and of distress for God's people Israel. He sees in that distress both Divine chastening and human persecution. The reference may be to the believing remnant rather than to the guilty masses who brought on the captivity and its sufferings. The prophet says that in their distress they have sought the Lord in whispered prayer (vs. 16). They are urged to hide for a little while until the wrath is past; and while it does not say so directly, where else could they hide than by taking refuge in faith in the living God? The prophet predicts a day of deliverance for God's people and of judgment upon them who have persecuted them and have shed innocent blood. The details of the historical background are not altogether clear; but both God's judgment upon persecutors and the purging effect of persecution in the life of God's people can be seen in the text; and above all the emphasis is on God as the only sufficient help in every time of trouble.

There is a Jewish tradition to the effect that Isaiah himself suffered martyrdom under the wicked Manasseh, and that Hebrews 11:37 ("they were sawn in two") alludes to the manner of his death. The tradition cannot be proved, but it is certain that many of the prophets suffered persecution; and the words of Jesus in Matthew 23:34, 35, testify to the fact that there were martyrs for their faith in Israel as well as in the Christian Church. With this in mind the applicability of several phrases in the text to the general theme of the day should be evident.

Basic religious teachings of the text:

1. When in distress, seek the Lord in prayer.

2. Recognize that there may be an element of Divine chastening in every bitter experience of life, and let it draw to the Lord in faith rather than drive from Him in unbelief.

3. Look for an end to "the wrath" or "the indignation" that now causes so much blood to be shed in the earth.

New Testament echoes of the text:

1. Jesus uses the illustration of the woman in travail in John 16:21.

2. Whether verse 19a predicts a bodily resurrection or a spiritual regeneration the language is borrowed from the concept of resurrection.

3. The phrase "for a little moment" (vs. 20, ASV; "for a little while," RSV) reminds of Paul's similar phrase in II Corinthians 4:17, "for the moment" (ASV; "momentary," RSV). The similarity extends to the context.

4. The same concept of judgment phrased in somewhat similar language is to be seen in Isaiah 26:21 and Luke 11:50.

Sunday After Christmas

TOPIC FOR THE DAY: "The Childhood of Jesus."

TEXT: Isaiah 41:8-14

THEME: Fear not, child of God!

Relation of the text to the topic:

There is a dual theme in the lessons for this Sunday. The Old Gospel text from Luke 2:33-40 speaks of the childhood of Jesus, the Son of God. The Old Epistle text from Galatians 4:1-7 speaks also of Jesus' birth and human status; but it enlarges the picture to include our status as children of God through "adoption as sons."

There is a close kinship between the Messiah and his people. The Son of God and the children of God have certain experiences in common. In Exodus 4:22 and in Hosea 11:1 Israel is called "my son." In some of the servant-passages of Isaiah, Israel is also called "my servant." That is true in Isaiah 41:8. But the things said of Israel are said of her in the ideal sense, or insofar as she conformed to the spiritual character and was true to the spiritual mission that were fundamental to the covenant of blessing with Abraham and with Israel. Jesus, as a Jew according to the flesh, and as a member of the covenant nation, shared that character and fulfilled that mission. What was said of Israel as God's son and servant can be applied to Jesus. The New Testament stresses the fact that Jesus as the Christ became a sharer with us in flesh and blood, in order that we might share with him the full status of children of God and also of servants of God. The second Gospel selection in the Augustana series, Luke 12:32, with the message, "Fear not, little flock," is a perfect parallel to Isaiah 41:8-14 with its wonderful promise to God's people.

Basic religious teachings of the text:

1. Israel, as the seed of Abraham, was called to be God's servant. This call to Israel includes the mission of the Messiah to be in the highest sense the servant of the Lord. It includes also the mission of the Christian Church which with Christ is called to serve God in the ministry of the gospel.

2. Fear not! Why not? Because of God's heart-warming promise to His people that He will stand by them in the service to which He has called them. He will be faithful to His covenant. He will strengthen and uphold and help His people. He will not cast them away if they look to Him as their God. He will deliver them from all their enemies. There are deep spiritual implications for God's people in every age in such a promise even though it also had reference at first (as the succeeding chapters indicate) to a redemption from captivity in Babylon.

3. The outstanding thoughts are the thrice-repeated statement, "I will help you," and the admonition, also thrice-repeated, "Fear not."

New Testament echoes of the text:

1. "The offspring of Abraham" (vs. 8; ASV, "the seed of Abraham") points backward to the promise in Genesis that "in thee and in thy seed shall all the nations of the earth be blessed" (ASV), and points forward to the truth stated in Galatians 3:29, "And if you are Christ's, then you are Abraham's offspring (ASV "seed"), heirs according to promise."

2. "Abraham, my friend" is echoed in James 2:23, "and he was called the friend of God."

3. The admonition, "fear not," occurs frequently in the New Testament. The reason for the admonition given in vs. 10, "for I am with you," reminds of Romans 8:31, the same reason in a different setting.

4. "I have chosen you and not cast you off" (vs. 9) is much like Jesus' reassuring promise in John 6:37.

New Year's Day

Topic for the Day: "The Name of Jesus."

Text: Isaiah 7:10-16

Theme: Jesus, our Immanuel! (or, Immanuel, God with us).

Relation of the text to the topic:

On this eighth day of Christmas the Old Gospel text, Luke 2:21, commemorates the circumcision of the Christ-child, at which time "he was called Jesus." The real theme for the day, therefore, is the name of JESUS. This name was not given to the Messiah by the Old Testament prophets. It was given by the angel Gabriel. Among the names prophetically given to the Messiah is the name IMMANUEL. Both names are descriptive or "telling" names, which unveil to us something of the significance of the character and of the coming of the Christ. The name fits the person. The name is descriptive of the function of the one to whom it is given. The names "Jesus" and "Immanuel" are essentially one in meaning. The name Jesus is etymologically a Latinized form of the Greek Iesous, which stands for the Hebrew Jeshua or Joshua, meaning "Jehovah is salvation." The name Immanuel means "God with us." The lessons for this day stress not only the truth of salvation through Jesus Christ our Saviour but also the related thought of the gracious presence of God with His people. The latter makes a splendid spiritual keynote for the beginning of another new year.

The name Immanuel is a beautiful and a meaningful word even when it stands by itself alone; but we should remember that it comes to us out of the Bible as a part of a wide Scriptural context, which we need to see and to understand if we are to understand the meaning of Jesus our Immanuel. It is related to the covenant promise in Genesis 17:7, 8, "I will be their God," and to the corollary promise in Exodus 19:5, "Ye shall be Mine own treasure from among all peoples" (ASV). It is related to the spiritual symbolism of the tabernacle as a meeting-place between God and His people, Exodus 25:22, and to the covenant concept of a God who dwells among His people, Exodus 29:45,46. It is related to the phrase "my presence" in Exodus 33:14-16; see also "his own presence," Deuteronomy 4:37, and "the angel of his presence," Isaiah 63:9. The truth that it represents is the very foundation of the covenant of blessing with Abraham and with us. It expresses an eternal covenant principle. This truth could have been experienced by King Ahaz in that definite historical situation when the prophet confronted him with the sign and the name of Immanuel (see Isaiah 7:14, and also 8:8,10), but he rejected it in unbelief. This truth applies to us as God's people today, if with all our heart we truly seek Him. But it is in Jesus Christ as the Incarnate Son of God that this truth found, and finds, its fullest expression. We believe that the prophet speaks here of the Messiah, who is Immanuel in the fullest sense of the word.

Basic religious teachings of the text:

1. The hypocritical unbelief of Ahaz, which wearies God but does not weaken His faithfulness to His covenant purpose.

2. The spiritually heartening promise implied in the name Immanuel; the truth of the presence of God with His people wherever and whenever they seek Him in spirit and truth.

3. The prediction of Messiah as Immanuel, through whom the tabernacle of God is now and ever shall be with men (John 1:14; Revelation 21:3-4). The New Testament makes it clear that there is such a prediction. In its phrasing the prediction conforms to the prophetic practice which so often "reveals" and "conceals" at the same time. The fulfilment is needed to make fully clear what lay in the prediction.

New Testament echoes of the text:

1. The clearest reference is in Matthew 1:22, 23, which claims fulfilment of Isaiah 7:14 in the virgin birth of Jesus Christ to be the Saviour of his people from their sins.

2. The covenant concept of the presence of God finds its ultimate fulfilment in the Incarnation. Whether it be the Immanuel prophecy, or the tabernacle as a dwelling-place of God, or the angel of His presence, or the covenant promise to be "their God," there is a foreshadowing of the time when "God was in Christ, reconciling the world to himself." The Incarnation brought the truth of Immanuel, God with us, to its full and final fruition.

3. There is an essential oneness between the promise in the name Immanuel, God with us, and the personal promise of Jesus who is our Immanuel, "Lo, I am with you always, to the close of the age" (Matthew 28:20).

Sunday After New Year

Topic for the Day: "The Baptism of Jesus."

Text: Isaiah 42:1-9.

Theme: Behold, my servant!

Relation of the text to the topic:

The texts for this Sunday differ greatly in various lectionaries. In the Augustana lectionary there is a dual theme in the lessons as there was for the Sunday after Christmas. The Old Gospel text from Matthew 3:13-17 speaks of the baptism of Jesus by John. The Old Epistle text from Romans 6:3-11 speaks of our baptism, or of Christian baptism as instituted by Jesus. Other texts for the day have this in common that they all refer to baptism: the meaning of Christian baptism as communion with Christ, the baptism of the Ethiopian eunuch by Philip, and the witness of John concerning the baptism of Jesus. The point of unity between them can be seen in the significance of baptism as a consecration. For Jesus his baptism marked the formal consecration or "anointing" to his Messianic ministry of redemption. For us baptism is an entering into communion with Christ through the new birth, which means also our consecration to a new life.

The lesson from Isaiah does not speak specifically of baptism, but it does speak of the consecration of the Christ as the servant of God. This is one of the servant-passages which seems to be a direct personal reference to the Messiah. Its opening announcement, "Behold, my servant, whom I uphold, my chosen, in whom my soul delights," is strikingly similar to the words of the voice from heaven at Jesus' baptism, "This is my beloved Son, with whom I am well pleased" (Matthew 3: 17). The statement, "I have put my Spirit upon him," is in full harmony with the declaration in Matthew 3:16 that "he saw the Spirit of God descending like a dove, and alighting on him." The whole context of Isaiah 42:1-7 is interpreted by Peter in Acts 10:38, "how God anointed Jesus of Nazareth with the Holy Spirit and with power; how he went about doing good and healing all that were oppressed by the devil, for God was with him." The story of the Ethiopian is a living illustration of the function of the servant to be "a light to the nations." It is this element of consecration, or of anointing to a God-given mission, together with the reassuring promise of God to be with His servant and to hold his hand and to uphold him, that applies with equal fitness to Jesus' own baptism or to ours. That is, it applies to ours if we understand Christian baptism in the correct Scriptural sense in which Luther relates it to the whole of the Christian life. See Luther's Small Catechism, "What does such baptizing with water signify?"

Basic religious teachings of the text:

1. The servant concept; the Divine call and the personal consecration to a holy service.

2. The spiritual ministry of the Messiah, the servant of the Lord (vs. 6-7); a ministry inclusive in scope (a covenant to the people, a light to the nations), and a ministry whose object is "redemption and release" from spiritual as well as physical blindness and imprisonment and bondage.

3. The tender sympathy and patience of the Messiah's ministry (vs. 3), so strikingly seen in the life of Christ; a spirit which should also characterize the ministry of his church.

4. The quietness of the spiritual appeal of God's servant (vs. 2), with none of the noisiness of the demagogue.

5. The power unto victory of the Messiah (vs. 4).

New Testament echoes of the text:

1. In Matthew 12:15-21 the words of the prophet in Isaiah 42:1-4 are said to have been fulfilled in the teaching and healing ministry of Jesus, which was carried on without fanfare or seeking after publicity.

2. The reference to the Messiah as "my servant" is reflected in the Book of Acts, where Jesus on several occasions is called "His Servant" (Acts 3:13, 26; 4:27, 30). The same concept of Jesus as servant occurs in Philippians 2:7. Jesus stressed the concept in Matthew 20:26-28, in relation both to himself and to his disciples.

3. Peter's reference to Christ as "a cornerstone chosen and precious" (I Peter 2:4, 6) reflects Isaiah 28:16, in the first instance, but it certainly includes also the concept of "my chosen."

4. The acknowledgment concerning the servant, "in whom my soul delights," is very similar to the acknowledgment concerning the Son, "with whom I am well pleased" (Matthew 3:17; 17:5). The New Testa-

ment quotation of the second line of Isaiah 42:1 in Matthew 12:18 resembles even more the words of Divine approval at his baptism and
on the Mount of Transfiguration, "my beloved with whom my soul is
well pleased."

5. For the reference to the Spirit in relation to the servant (vs. 1)
there are numerous parallels in the New Testament, beginning with
the scene of Jesus' baptism and including Peter's statement in Acts 10:
38. Some of these parallel passages may refer more directly to Isaiah
61:1, but the basic concept is the same as in Isaiah 42:1. RSV incon-
sistently has "spirit" in Isaiah 42:1 while capitalizing the word in the
quotation in Matthew 12:18. There can be no question but that the
reference is to the Divine Spirit.

6. The twofold aspect of the servant's work, in relation to the people
of Israel and to the Gentiles, is echoed in the Nunc Dimittis, Luke 2:32,
and in Romans 15.

7. The opening of the blind eyes (vs. 7) is illustrated both physically
and spiritually in the ministry of Jesus. The release from the prison-
house of sin is the very essence of the salvation that he came to accomplish.

Epiphany

Topic for the Day: "The Dawn of a New Day."

Text: Isaiah 2:2-5

Theme: A light for revelation to the Gentiles.

Relation of the text to the topic:

The word Epiphany means to become manifest. It suggests the un-
veiling of the glory of God in Christ. It is therefore intimately connected with the spiritual concept of light and of the dawn of a new
day, as when Jesus said, "I am the light of the world: he who follows
me will not walk in darkness, but will have the light of life" (John 8:
12). If he is the light of the world he must also be the light of the
Gentiles. The lessons for Epiphany give special emphasis to the minis-

try of Christ in relation to the Gentiles. We see it in the gospel story of the coming of the Wise-men from the east to seek the new-born King of the Jews. We see it in the prophecy of Isaiah that "in the latter days" all nations shall seek the Lord, and shall be taught of Him, and shall walk in His ways.

This is a missionary text. That is one reason why it is a good Epiphany text. Though the personal Messiah is not to be seen in the prophecy the fulfilment of the prophecy began with Jesus Christ and continues through the missionary efforts of the Christian Church. The invitation in Isaiah 2:5 was pertinent in its own day, for God had begun even then to let His light shine among men through the revelation given in the law and the prophets. The invitation is even more pertinent now when through the preaching of the gospel all men are urged to walk in "the light of the knowledge of the glory of God in the face of Jesus Christ" (II Corinthians 4:6). The covenant with Abraham sounded this universal note from the beginning: "in thee shall all the families of the earth be blessed" (Genesis 12:3, ASV).

The same universal note is frequent in the book of Isaiah. This fact is sufficient to account for the prominent place of the book of Isaiah in the lessons for Epiphany. The Old Epistle text is from Isaiah 60:1-6. The lesson from Isaiah 2:2-5 is included in the Augustana lectionary and in the Eisenach Old Testament selections. Both the Augustana and the ELC lectionaries include as a third Gospel Matthew 12:15-21, which contains a significant quotation from Isaiah 42, our text for the Sunday after New Year. In the ELC lectionary Isaiah 49:1-6 is used as the third series Epistle. This may serve to indicate the flexibility with which some of the messages from Isaiah can be used, as well as the close connection in thought and emphasis between Christmas, New Year, and Epiphany.

Basic religious teachings of the text:

1. The prediction of a glorious future exaltation of the mountain of the house of the LORD. This is the language of religious symbolism. The exaltation of the mountain on which stood the house of Jehovah is the symbol of the coming exaltation and preeminence of the religion of Jehovah. In the light of history this can be seen to be the preeminence of Jesus Christ, and of Christianity. It is the preeminence of Christ (Colossians 1:18) which gives to Christianity its unique place as a religion with a gospel and a way of life that cannot be excelled.

2. The missionary process that shall lead to the final victory of Christ and of the religion of Jehovah through and in him. The heathen nations are represented as seeking, and inviting one another to seek, the God of Israel. In the light of history this can be seen to be the great missionary movement that since the coming of Christ has been drawing men to him through the preaching of the gospel. It results in the conversion of the Gentiles, who share in the covenant blessing with Abraham, as Paul says in Galatians 3:14.

3. The drawing and motivating power in this missionary movement is the Torah, or the Law, here seen in its original sense as the teaching of the Word of God which reveals His good and gracious will with respect to men, including the gospel of our salvation.

4. The result will be peace. We know that the effect of the gospel is peace; first, with God, and then, with this as an effective basis, peace among men. It is of the latter that the prophet speaks here (vs. 4). But though the emphasis is on the latter, the former is not thereby excluded. Let us be careful lest in our emphasis on the former we exclude the latter. Peace on earth hovers before us as a promise of Almighty God.

5. The invitation to walk now in the light given us by God in His Word.

New Testament echoes of the text:

There is no quotation from this text in the New Testament, nor any direct claim that it has been fulfilled; but it is not difficult to see the relationship between prophecy and history. There is a fulfilment of this prophecy to be seen in the New Testament as well as in the continuing history of the Christian Church. The fulfilment can be seen in the preeminence of Christ, in the excellency of the gospel and of the Christian way of life, in the conversion of the Gentiles, in the supreme revelation of God who at the end of these days has spoken unto us in His Son, and in the spiritual experience of peace which is a promise and a foretaste of peace in the all-inclusive sense in which the prophets speak of it.

Epiphany

TOPIC FOR THE DAY: "The Dawn of a New Day."

TEXT: Isaiah 60:1-9.

THEME: Arise, shine; for your light is come!

Relation of the text to the topic:

The unifying word in the lessons for Epiphany is *light,* and the unifying thought is the coming of the nations to this light which shines first upon Zion.

Isaiah 60 must be seen against the background of chapter 59 with its graphic confession of national wickedness. The antithesis of light is darkness. Darkness is a symbol of sin and of judgment, of spiritual ignorance and of spiritual apostasy. In chapter 59 the prophet speaks of the darkness of Israel's apostasy and resulting affliction: "Your iniquities have made a separation between you and your God, and your sins have hid his face from you so that he does not hear" (vs. 2), with the result that "we look for light, and behold darkness, and for brightness, but we walk in gloom" (vs. 9). In chapter 60, verse 2, he speaks of a darkness of ignorance which covers the peoples of the whole earth. But into this situation of darkness a Redeemer will come (ch. 59:20). With the coming of the Redeemer comes also light. It is the light of the knowledge of the glory of God, which becomes the glory of His people because it includes His acknowledgment of them in saving mercy and righteousness.

Though the Messiah is not mentioned by name in this chapter we must say with Dummelow, that "this prophecy received its highest fulfilment at the coming of Christ, the true light of the world, which was followed by a great ingathering of the nations to the Church of God." The words of Simeon in the Nunc Dimittis, Luke 2:30-32, are a perfect parallel to the words of the prophet, except that the words light and glory as Isaiah uses them seem to be synonyms, but as Simeon uses them there is a shade of difference between the two: the Christ is a light of revelation to the heathen because he comes to them as to those without knowledge of God, living in the darkness of spiritual ignorance; and he is the glory of his people Israel, because he is himself an

Israelite, and he fulfils in himself the glorious covenant promises given to them from the time of Abraham. But to both Jew and Gentile, or to all men everywhere, he comes as the light that can illumine the minds and hearts of those who otherwise walk in darkness and despair. This is another true Epiphany text because it is a true missionary text. It is a true Epiphany text because it speaks of the revelation of the glory of God in Christ, and in His people also, as they let the light shine.

Basic religious teachings of the text:

1. The Messianic prediction which, without mentioning the Messiah by name, looks forward to that which took place when he came into the world to save his people from their sins and to let all men see in him the glory of the only-begotten from the Father, full of grace and truth (John 1:14).

2. The concept of spiritual light in all its New Testament fulness.

3. The concept of the glory of God, so prominent in the book of Isaiah from chapter 6:3 on, and so closely related to his people, upon whom the glory is risen (vs. 1, 2, 9).

4. The radiance and the joy of God's people as they see the nations come to share in the light and to unite in proclaiming the praises of the Lord (vs. 4-6).

5. The missionary duty to be a light, and to let our light shine (vs. 1). Jesus, who said, "I am the light of the world," also said, "You are the light of the world": therefore "Arise, shine!"

New Testament echoes of the text:

1. "Your light" and "the glory of the LORD" (vs. 1-3) remind us of the language in II Corinthians 4:6. We see the full light of the knowledge of the glory of God in the face of Jesus Christ.

2. The concept of darkness (vs. 2) is similar in import to the Pauline teaching concerning "the dominion of darkness" from which we have been delivered, Colossians 1:13. See also Acts 26:18, "that they may turn from darkness to light"; John 1:5, "the light shines in the darkness"; Ephesians 5:8, "for once you were darkness, but now you are light in the Lord"; and I Peter 2:9, "who called you out of darkness into his marvelous light."

3. The statement in Ephesians 1:12, "we who first hoped in Christ have been destined and appointed to live for the praise of his glory,"

sums up the thought in Isaiah 60 of a redeemed people that shall see the glory of the Lord upon them, and shall proclaim the praises of the LORD (vs. 6).

4. The house of the LORD was indeed glorified (vs. 7) by the presence of Jesus Christ, the Lord of glory (I Corinthians 2:8).

First Sunday After Epiphany

TOPIC FOR THE DAY: "Jesus as Disciple and Teacher."

TEXT: Isaiah 50:4-10.

THEME: The tongue of those who are taught.

Relation of the text to the topic:

Our text is one of those wherein Christian faith has seen a prophetic picture of our Lord Jesus Christ in his suffering as the faithful and obedient servant of the Lord. It would make an excellent text for a series of Lenten sermons; but it makes just as good a text for the first Sunday after Epiphany. The Old Gospel text for this day is the story of Jesus in the temple at the age of twelve, when we see him as a disciple, or learner, with unusual promise as a future teacher of Israel. Luke 2:51 stresses his obedience as a child. Luke 2:52 describes his progress as a learner in these words: "And Jesus increased in wisdom and in stature, and in favor with God and man." Other texts give emphasis to the position of Jesus as teacher, and to his oneness with us as his brethren, so that he as a child and as a man shared our experience, and we in turn may learn from the human experience of Jesus.

In our text from the book of Isaiah we see the Servant as a disciple (vs. 4), who has been given "the tongue of those who are taught" (see ASV mg., "disciples"). He is a disciple because he has been taught by God. The purpose and the result of the instruction given him is that he might teach others also, or that he might know "how to sustain with a word him that is weary" (See ASV mg., "to speak a word in season to him that is weary"). We see faithfulness as a disciple in learning "morning by morning" (vs. 4b). We see also the attitude of firm obedience in the face of suffering and scorn, which may have come his way both as a learner and as a teacher (vs. 5-6). This is no mere mental exercise in learning a lesson by rote from a book. This is a lesson that must be lived out, and that is not learned until it is lived; and the Servant is willing to live as he has been taught, in spite of suffering and shame. We see the Servant's assurance of the presence and the help of God (vs. 7a, 9a), which enables him to show forth firmness in faith and duty, setting his face like a flint to the task appointed to him, and knowing that he will not be put to shame in his confidence in God (vs. 7). We see the Servant's confident hope of eventual justification or vindication by God against any and every adversary (vs. 8, 9). We see him who though he was a Son as well as a servant "learned obedience through what he suffered" (Hebrews 5:8); and the lesson to us is this, that we learn from him to fear God, and to obey, and to trust in the name of the Lord our God, even though we walk in the darkness of the valley of the shadow of death.

Basic religious teachings of the text:

1. We need to be taught by the Lord.

2. Being taught, we can teach others also, and with our teaching sustain the weary, who need to know God.

3. One who is truly taught of God is obedient, not rebellious; the knowledge of God leads to right action; the lesson is translated into life.

4. One who lives as taught of God is likely to encounter scorn and shame even as did the Lord Jesus Christ.

5. One who puts his trust in God and faithfully serves Him at whatever cost shall not be put to shame. God is near. God will help. God will justify and not condemn, if we fear, love, and trust in Him.

New Testament echoes of the text:

1. The ministry of the Servant, "to sustain with a word him that is weary," is exemplified in the invitation of Jesus, "Come to me, all who labor and are heavy-laden, and I will give you rest" (Matthew 11:28-30), and in his entire ministry.

2. The attitude of obedience on the part of the Servant was the attitude also of the Son. See Matthew 26:39; John 4:34; John 6:38; Philippians 2:8; Hebrews 5:8; Romans 5:19.

3. The smiting and the spitting in the case of the Servant was dupli-
cated in the experience of Jesus in the court of Caiaphas and in the
palace of Pilate, with the same meek submission on the part of the
sufferer.

4. The statement in verse 7, "therefore have I set my face like a
flint," reminds of the statement in Luke 9:51, that "when the days drew
near for him to be received up, he set his face to go to Jerusalem."
There is in both the same steadfast devotion to duty, the same firm consecration to a God-given task.

5. The language of Romans 8:33, 34, is partly borrowed from Isaiah
50:8, 9. The prophet speaks of the justification or vindication of the
Servant, whom we understand to be the Messiah. The apostle applies
the words to the justification of the believer in Christ. There is no
contradiction. God's vindication of Christ and acceptance of his work of
redemption leads to our justification for the sake of Christ.

Second Sunday After Epiphany

TOPIC FOR THE DAY: "The Manifestation of Jesus as Messiah."
TEXT: Isaiah 61:1-6.
THEME: That you may believe that Jesus is the Christ.

Relation of the text to the topic:

The Augustana lectionary suggests as the general topic for the day,
"The Presence of Jesus Hallows the Home." It is an appropriate topic,
for several of the texts are indeed related to the home, and to the presence or to the influence of Jesus within it. The Old Gospel is the story
of the wedding in Cana, where Jesus honored the home with his presence and hallowed the occasion with a sign which manifested his glory.
Both the Augustana and the ELC lectionaries include as additional
lessons the stories of Jesus and the Samaritan woman, and of Jesus in
the home of Zacchaeus.

In all three of the lessons listed, however, we see also the manifestation of Jesus as Messiah. The statement in John 2:11, "This, the first of his signs, Jesus did at Cana in Galilee, and manifested his glory; and his disciples believed in him," reminds of the statement in John 20:30, 31, as to the purpose with the signs which Jesus did and which are written in this book, "that you may believe that Jesus is the Christ, the Son of God, and that believing you may have life in his name." The Samaritan woman was convinced by Jesus' words of the truth of his claim that he was the Messiah. To Zacchaeus he came with salvation and in so doing revealed himself to be indeed the Christ.

Bo Giertz, in his book "Grunden," says that the Epiphany theme is "the revelation (or manifestation) of the glory of Jesus," and that the theme for the Sundays after Epiphany is "the activity of Jesus in Galilee." The emphasis throughout the Epiphany season, and especially on the Second Sunday after Epiphany is on the words and works of Jesus which give evidence of his Messiahship. From this point of view the prophetic picture of Messiah's activity in Isaiah 61 is an ideal text for the day. It was the text for Jesus' sermon at Nazareth, wherein he said, "Today this scripture has been fulfilled in your hearing" (Luke 4: 16-21. It is the selection of the Eisenach Old Testament series for this Sunday. The preacher should have no difficulty in relating it also to the home if he so desires; for it is when Jesus is known as the Christ by every family member that his presence truly hallows the home.

Basic religious teachings of the text:

1. The anointing of the Messiah with the Holy Spirit to equip him for his work; a frequent concept in the book of Isaiah. See Isaiah 11:2; 42:1; and 59:21, where it is related to God's people.

2. The preaching of good tidings or good news (the gospel) as the first and foremost objective in the Messiah's ministry.

3. The Messiah's concern for the poor (in whatever sense), for the broken-hearted (from whatever cause), for the captive and imprisoned (in sin or in any other form of human bondage): in short, for those in need (temporal or spiritual).

4. The combination of the salvation and judgment motifs in Messiah's ministry; but with primary emphasis on favor and joy and righteousness and praise.

5. The function of God's redeemed people to be "priests of the Lord" or "ministers of our God," in accordance with the original covenant purpose. See Exodus 19:6.

New Testament echoes of the text:

1. The primary reference is in Luke 4:16-21, where Jesus quotes the first verse and a part of the second in free translation, and makes the claim that it was being fulfilled at that very moment.

2. The spirit of the ministry of the Messiah as portrayed by the prophet is clearly comparable to the spirit seen in the ministry of Jesus, both in his teaching and in his healing ministry.

3. The Messiah's mission, "to comfort all who mourn," reminds of the Beatitude, "Blessed are those who mourn, for they shall be comforted," Matt. 5:4.

4. The spiritual priesthood spoken of in verse 6 looks backward to Exodus 19:6 and forward to I Peter 2:9. Whether under the Old Covenant or the New, the purpose of salvation is that there might be service and praise, that God might be glorified.

5. "The ministers of our God" is a phrase reminiscent of many New Testament passages which emphasize the position of the Christian as a minister or a servant.

Third Sunday After Epiphany

TOPIC FOR THE DAY: "Jesus the Creator of Faith."

TEXT: Isaiah 43:1-7.

THEME: Fear not, only believe!

Relation of the text to the topic:

The Epiphany theme of "the manifestation of the glory of Jesus the Messiah" continues in the texts for this Sunday. It is closely connected with the theme of *faith.* Because of the works that he did, and because of the words that they heard him speak, many believed on him. That was true of the Roman centurion who asked Jesus to heal his servant (Matthew 8:1-13). His faith was based on what he had heard about the works of healing that Jesus did. It was a remarkable faith, which caused even Jesus to marvel, and to see in this man a representative of the many that should come from the Gentiles into the covenant with Abraham and into the kingdom of heaven. In the continuation of the story of the Samaritan woman (John 4), many of the Samaritans believed on him; first, because of the word of the woman, and then because of his own word. "They said to the woman, 'It is no longer because of your words that we believe, for we have heard for ourselves, and we know that this is indeed the Saviour of the world'" (John 4:42).

Jesus is indeed the creator of faith, just as in the Old Testament the LORD, the Redeemer of Israel, is seen as the creator of faith. There is strong encouragement to faith in the words spoken to Israel in our text from Isaiah 43: "Fear not, for I have redeemed you" (vs. 1); "fear not, for I am with you" (vs. 5); "for I am the LORD your God, the Holy One of Israel, your Saviour" (vs. 3). The words of the prophet must be seen first in their Old Testament setting, as addressed to Israel. The full truth of "God in Christ" is not revealed here, but it is nevertheless the God and Father of our Lord Jesus Christ who speaks. The full spiritual meaning of redemption is not to be seen here; but the redemption from Egypt, and from Babylon, are related both historically and spiritually to the "eternal redemption" through the blood of Christ. It is the living covenant God who speaks in each situation, and who through His "fear not" creates faith. Though not strictly a prophecy of the Messiah the spiritual principles here enunciated in the form of Divine promises of Israel can be rightfully applied to Christ and put on his lips as promises to the New Testament seed of Abraham. Many other texts in the book of Isaiah speak the same message of "fear not, only believe," and can be used by God's people now as a word from God to them; for God does not change.

Basic religious teachings of the text:

1. The recognition of God's activity in history, whereby He calls nations (vs. 1) and individuals (vs. 7), as a truly Divine work, which can be likened to a work of creation. The purpose with the reminder that "I have created you" is to create faith in God as the One who is able to redeem and to protect His own.

2. The encouragement to faith: "Fear not, for I have redeemed you" (vs. 1); "fear not, for I am with you" (vs. 5).

3. The tender, intimately personal relationship of God to His people under the covenant: "I have called you by name, you are mine" (vs. 1). See Exodus 19:5, "my own possession," "my priceless treasure."

4. The promise of God's presence with and protection for His people in every time of need (vs. 2). The language is figurative; the experience is real.

5. The designation and description of God as "the LORD your God, the Holy One of Israel, your Saviour" (vs. 3) is still true in relation to the New Testament Church. The Old Testament theology is always richly relevant for our faith.

6. The emphasis on God's love as motivating His action: "Because you are precious in my eyes, and honored, and I love you—" (vs. 4).

7. The prophetic promise of a return and a restoration of Israel from their far-reaching dispersion, as a part of God's ultimate realization of the goal of His redemptive activity and of His covenant with Abraham.

New Testament echoes of the text:

1. Direct quotation there is none; except possibly in the composite passage of II Corinthians 6:17, 18, where the last line, "and you shall be my sons and daughters," may reflect Isaiah 43:6, "bring my sons from afar and my daughters from the end of the earth." The Hosea passage, which is a part of the quotation by Paul, speaks only of *sons.* The reference to *daughters* may be borrowed from Isaiah 43. Two things are interesting in Paul's use of prophecy here: first, that he quotes prophecy with literary freedom, not hesitating to change the wording and to combine widely separated sentences; and secondly, that he looks beneath the surface of the prediction, which in this instance is a prediction of an earthly restoration of Israel from exile to the promised land and to renewed covenant fellowship with their God, and gets at the spiritual principle involved applying it to the break with heathenism that was so urgently needed at Corinth if they were to be indeed God's people, God's children.

2. The "fear not" of this chapter has frequent parallels in the New Testament as well as in the Old Testament.

3. "I am with you" (vs. 5) is a basic motif of the covenant of blessing with Abraham. As used here the statement is reminiscent of Psalm

23:4, "I fear no evil; for thou art with me." It reminds also of the promise of Jesus, "I am with you always" (Matthew 28:20).

4. The reference to God as "your Saviour" has many New Testament parallels. See "God our Saviour," I Timothy 1:1 and 2:3; Titus 1:3; 2:10 and 3:4; and Jude 25. See also "God my Saviour," Luke 1:47.

Fourth Sunday After Epiphany

TOPIC FOR THE DAY: "Jesus Delivers from Danger and Despair."
TEXT: Isaiah 40:26-31.
THEME: The power of God is the strength of His people.

Relation of the text to the topic:

One of the Epistles for this Sunday according to several lectionaries is II Timothy 1:7-10. The opening sentence strikes the keynote of all the texts for the day: "For God did not give us a spirit of timidity but a spirit of power and love and self-control." The stilling of the tempest and the walking on the sea manifested the power of Jesus in the physical realm; and it reacted on the disciples in the realm of the spirit by creating faith instead of fearfulness. Faith gives power, spiritual and moral power; the power to cope with life, in the assurance that God is with us.

The prayer in the Collect is pertinent: "O Lord, our heavenly Father, who knowest us to be set in the midst of so many and great dangers that by the reason of the frailty of our nature we cannot always stand upright; grant us such strength and protection as will support us in all dangers, and carry us through all temptations." It is of such strength and strengthening that Isaiah speaks in our text. Addressed to Israel in their time of adversity and affliction, when it seemed to them that their way was hid from God, and that God neither saw nor cared what happened to them, its purpose is to direct their faith again to God, "the everlasting God, the Creator of the ends of the earth," who is not faint and weary and helpless *now* in life's situations. He gives power to the faint, and increases strength to those who have no might of their own. There is but one condition, and that is that we wait for the LORD in humble prayer and faith. In fact, the whole chapter presupposes a situation where God comforts a penitent people, that has been afflicted and chastened because of its sins, and now needs to be reassured that God has not forsaken them.

Every statement in the text, though spoken first to Israel in a specific historical situation, speaks with equal directness to us. The message is as timeless as God Himself. "They who wait for the LORD shall renew their strength, they shall mount up with wings like eagles, they shall run and not be weary, they shall walk and not faint."

Basic religious teachings of the text:

1. The God of creation is also the God of history: His power is adequate in the one situation as in the other.

2. Our way in life is not hid from God, so that He does not see nor care what becomes of us, nor is He helpless to save us. Even when chastened and afflicted we may seek out and know His strength to enable us to endure.

3. The theology of verse 28 is sublime: "The LORD is the everlasting God, the Creator of the ends of the earth. He does not faint or grow weary, his understanding is unsearchable."

4. When life becomes too difficult even for the young, so that they become faint and weary with discouragement, our one source of refuge and strength is in the living God. Wait for Him! He will renew and increase faith and courage, giving that spiritual and moral strength which is of far more importance than the purely physical. Faith in the living God gives power, and not a spirit of fearfulness.

New Testament echoes of the text:

1. There is a marked similarity between this text and the parable of Jesus in Luke 18:1-8. Jesus spoke the parable "to the effect that they ought always to pray and not lose heart" (ASV, "not to faint"). The prophet encouraged his people to wait for the Lord in prayer, that they might not faint. The prophet forcefully rejected the idea that "my way is hid from the Lord, and my right is disregarded by my God." Jesus just as definitely asserted the positive side of the case when he said: "And will not God vindicate his elect, who cry to him day and night? Will he delay long over them? I tell you, he will vindicate them

speedily." In both cases the vital importance of faith is emphasized. The prophet seeks to encourage faith. Jesus closes the parable by asking, "Nevertheless, when the Son of man comes, will he find faith on earth?"

2. The theology of verse 28, especially the closing statement that "his understanding is unsearchable," is clearly the same as in Romans 11:33.

3. Jesus' words of invitation in Matthew 11:25-30 have much in common with the passage from Isaiah 40; for rest and strength are closely associated.

4. The concept of strength in place of faintness is prominent in II Corinthians 4, and also in Hebrews 12. It is God who strengthens. Faith in the living God, which includes the "assurance of things hoped for, the conviction of things not seen" (Hebrews 11:1), gives power to live as God's children.

Fifth Sunday After Epiphany

TOPIC FOR THE DAY: "The Power of Jesus to Keep His Own."

TEXT: Isaiah 8:9-20.

THEME: God is our sanctuary (or, God is our refuge and strength).

Relation of the text to the topic:

The Epiphany theme continues, but with this difference, that in the lessons for this Sunday the manifestation of Jesus' glory as the Messiah comes through his word or teaching rather than through his works of power. The Old Epistle text from Colossians 3:12-17 admonishes us, "Let the word of Christ dwell in you richly" (vs. 16). The Old Gospel text is the parable of the wheat and the tares from Matthew 13:24-30; and the interpretation of the seed as the word (Mark 4:14) would seem to apply here also. Another lesson, from I Corinthians 1:9-18, emphasizes the word of the cross as foolishness to them that perish, but as the power of God to us who are saved.

The power of Jesus to save and to keep his own is exercised through his word, through the gospel, through the word of the cross. So also in our text from Isaiah God's people are directed to the LORD as their sanctuary in time of danger and distress, and to the law and the testimony, or to the word of God, as their only safe guide. The prophetic word bids them fear and trust in the LORD, and in the promise of Immanuel, "God is with us," and not to fear any human conspiracy or human aggression. The message was for the time of Ahaz, and of the conspiracy between Syria and Ephraim against Judah (vs. 12 in the light of ch. 7:1, and of the Assyrian invasion to which Ahaz helped open the door by his misdirected politics. The message is just as relevant for us today. There is no security for us either as individuals or as a nation if we leave God out of our planning and shut our ears to His word. There is security if "God is with us," as He will be if we are concerned to be with Him.

Basic religious teachings of the text:

1. The truth of Immanuel, "God is with us," is the only effective reply of God's people, singly and collectively, to the aggression of their enemies, temporal or spiritual.

2. The antidote to paralyzing human fears in such a time as ours is a true childlike faith and fear directed towards God as the LORD of hosts.

3. If we do not let God be a sanctuary to us He will become to us instead a stone of stumbling.

4. The importance of the word of God, the Torah and the testimony of the Old Testament, and the law and the gospel of the New Testament, as revealing Him who alone can be the sure foundation of our faith in every time of need, and as showing us His good will concerning the way in which we should walk.

5. Rejection of God's plainly spoken word of truth and direction leads to darkness, for a nation, for an individual; a darkness which is at first spiritual and moral, and then becomes the darkness of Divine judgment and of human affliction.

New Testament echoes of the text:

1. The question in Romans 8:31, "If God is for us, who is against us?" could be placed as a theme or heading over the message of the prophet. The truth is the same; though Isaiah sees it in reference to an earthly situation, such as the Assyrian invasion of the land of promise,

and Paul sees it in the more directly spiritual setting of the sinner's justification before God. In any situation, if God is with us, who can successfully be against us?

2. Isaiah's admonition with respect to a wrong and a right fear (vs. 12, 13) is echoed by Peter in a similar admonition to Christians (I Peter 3:14,15). The situation is different, but the principle is the same: fear God, do not be afraid of men.

3. The reference to "a stone of offence" and "a rock of stumbling" (vs. 14) is quoted in I Peter 2:8. The interpretation is that "they stumble because they disobey the word." In Romans 9:33 this same line from Isaiah 8:14 seems to be combined with a line from Isaiah 28:16, and the combined quotation is applied to Israel's failure to attain to true righteousness because they sought it not by faith but by works. The concept of stumbling over the stone is closely related to the concept of rejection of the stone; see Psalms 118:22. The Psalms passage is quoted in Matthew 21:42 and in Luke 20:17. In the application of the lesson Jesus uses the language of Isaiah 8:15. The point in common between Isaiah, Jesus, Peter, and Paul is that some stumble on the rock of the word of God in unbelief and disobedience. That was true of the prophetic word, and it is true of the word of the gospel of Jesus Christ. For such as disbelieve and disobey, God can be no sanctuary.

4. In Hebrews 2:13 words which the prophet speaks of himself in Isaiah 8:18 are represented as Christ's words about himself, "I and the children whom the Lord has given me." This is not a case of prediction, but it may be a borrowing of language to fit another situation.

5. The references to "signs and portents" in verse 18 has something in common with Simeon's words in Luke 2:34, "this child is set for the fall and rising of many in Israel, and for a sign that is spoken against." Such was the experience of both Isaiah and Jesus, and such was the effect of the ministry of both. There is a unity between the messenger and the Messiah that must not be overlooked in seeking to understand God's Word.

6. Jesus' words in the parable in Luke 16:29 are reminiscent of the words in Isaiah 8:20. There was enough light in God's Old Testament word for men to have faith and to be saved. There is certainly enough light in God's New Testament word for men to have faith and to be saved. If men will not believe on the basis of the word that is given it is not likely that any other word could persuade them to believe.

Septuagesima Sunday

TOPIC FOR THE DAY: "By Grace Alone."

TEXT: Isaiah 5:1-7.

THEME: What more was there to do for my vineyard, that I have not done in it?

Relation of the text to the topic:

Bo Giertz, in his book "Grunden," gives as the theme for Septuagesima and Sexagesima Sundays, "The teaching of Jesus about Grace and the Word."

The theme for Septuagesima is Grace. In the parable of the laborers in the vineyard, Matthew 20:1-16, Jesus stresses the privilege of working, without thought of pay, but with rich reward promised to all because God is good. There is a reward for following Christ and serving him, but it is a reward given by grace alone. Therefore in following Christ our thought should not be first about the reward, but rather about the privilege of serving him. God has a vineyard in which there is work to be done, and from which He looks for fruit; but it is of God's grace that we are privileged to work in this vineyard, and are enabled to bear fruit, and are entitled to a reward when the day's work is done. Such is the teaching of Jesus in his parable of the vineyard.

There is another parable of the vineyard which we may call Isaiah's. It makes a good text for Septuagesima Sunday because it resembles the Old Gospel text in being a parable of the vineyard. There is another and more significant point of resemblance in that Isaiah's parable like that of Jesus stresses God's grace. In His goodness and love God has done everything for His vineyard that could be done. A complete study of Old Testament history, and of God's gracious spiritual as well as temporal provision for His people within the covenant relationship, would illustrate the point. The vineyard in Isaiah's parable is identified for us as the house of Israel; but we can readily see the connection between God's Old Testament Israel and His New Testament Church. The expectation of good fruit from the vineyard is stated by Isaiah and implied by Jesus. God's disappointment with His vineyard because it did not yield the fruit of righteousness shows us that grace and good works are not incompatible; but grace comes first, by grace alone are we saved, and permitted to be a part of God's husbandry, and enabled to fulfill our calling to serve Him in righteousness and to accomplish His will.

Basic religious teachings of the text:

1. The care of God for His vineyard (vs. 2). The language is figurative, as befits a parable; the spiritual application of the whole principle of Divine care for His vineyard is easy to make.

2. The expectation of fruit; spiritual and moral fruit, such as God has a right to receive of His people who enjoy His grace and favor. Specifically, the fruit of justice and of righteousness in human relationships as evidence of a right relationship with God. Justice, or just judgment, and righteousness are two very important Biblical words. If our faith is reckoned to us for righteousness (Genesis 15:6), should not the fruit be seen in righteousness of life? If we are saved by grace alone, should not the result be grateful good works?

3. The disappointment of God in His expectation (vs. 7). What a glaring contrast: "he looked for justice, but behold, bloodshed; for righteousness, but behold, a cry!"

4. The judgment of God upon His vineyard which despised His grace (vs. 5, 6).

New Testament echoes of the text:

1. The language of Jesus in the parable of the wicked husbandmen, Matthew 21:33 ff., bears a marked resemblance to that of Isaiah and may be borrowed from him. The theme of this parable is also the same as Isaiah's, the failure of Israel as God's vineyard to bring forth fruit. This theme recurs frequently in the teaching of Jesus. See Luke 13:6-9, the parable of the fig tree planted in the vineyard; and Mark 11:12-14, the incident of the barren fig tree which Jesus cursed.

2. The question in Isaiah 5:4, "What more was there to do for my vineyard, that I have not done in it?" is closely parallel in thought to the lamentation in Matthew 23:37, "How often would I have gathered your children together—and you would not!"

3. The prediction that the vineyard shall be "trampled down" (ASV, "Trodden down") reminds of the statement in Luke 21:24 that "Jerusalem will be trodden down by the Gentiles."

4. The relationship between grace and good works which is implicit in this parable is made explicit in the teaching of the New Testament. Salvation is by grace, but God does seek good works as the fruit of faith.

Septuagesima Sunday

Another text that could be used for this Sunday is Isaiah 1:18-20. Verse 18 contains a challenge to a formal trial of the case at issue between God and His people (see preceding part of the chapter). The traditional interpretation of the verse is that God indicates that He will deal with the situation in compassionate grace, forgiveness, and cleansing. Repentance is not specifically mentioned but is presupposed by the willing obedience which is made a condition for their continuing to enjoy God's favor and to eat the good of the promised land. The sequence seems to be this: Divine grace is expressed in forgiveness and cleansing from sin, and this leads to obedience as an attitude of life. So interpreted it· illustrates perfectly the Septuagesima theme, "By grace alone."

Basic religious teachings of the text:

1. The invitation to talk things over with the Lord, or to reason together. He would reason with us in order that we might see what is true of us, that we have sinned, and what is good for us, that we should confess our sins and seek forgiveness and live in fellowship with Him in glad obedience of faith.

2. The assurance that we can experience the forgiveness of all our sins, however great they may be, and can become in God's sight "as white as snow."

3. The insistence on obedience as the right attitude of God's children on whom He bestows love and mercy. There is something tragically inconsistent in the situation described in Isaiah 1:2, "Sons have I reared and brought up, but they have rebelled against me." Even rebellion can be forgiven by our God, who is gracious and ready to forgive all who sincerely seek forgiveness; but forgiveness presupposes repentance, and repentance leads surely to obedience.

New Testament echoes of the text:

1. The cleansing from sin which makes us white as snow reminds of the still clearer but related statement in Revelation 7:14 concerning the white-robed host, "They have washed their robes, and made them white in the blood of the Lamb."

2. The tenderly pleading tone of this and other prophetic passages (for example, Micah 6:1-8) is very similar to that of Paul in Romans 12:1-2.

Sexagesima Sunday

Topic for the Day: "The Word of God."

Text: Isaiah 55:6-11.

Theme: "God's gracious word of invitation."

Relation of the text to the topic:

The keynote for this Sunday is sounded by this sentence from the parable of the sower and the seed, "The seed is the word of God" (Luke 8:11). All texts for the day speak either of the word or of the preaching of the word; and they speak of it as if it possessed life and power. The word is like a seed which, when planted, grows and bears fruit. The word is like a light by which we may walk and not stumble. The word can make us wise unto salvation. The word can furnish us completely unto every good work. The word is an announcement of the kingdom of heaven which is near. The word is an invitation. The word is a gospel, a message of good news.

It is not difficult to see why Isaiah 55:6-11 is admitted into such company and given a place in the Augustana lectionary as one of the lessons for Sexagesima; for it too speaks of God's word as a thing of life and power, which shall accomplish that which God pleases and shall prosper in the thing whereto God sends it (vs. 11). What kind of word is it? It is a word of gracious invitation to seek God while He may be found, and to experience His mercy and pardon. It is a word that reveals God as a God of infinite mercy and compassion. It is a word which truly exalts the love of God as being "broader than the measure of man's mind" (Frederick William Faber). It is the word of the gospel, glorious in its Old Testament dress, and more glorious still when seen "drawn out in living characters" in the life of Jesus Christ our Saviour. It is the power of God unto salvation to everyone that believes it. We almost lose sight of the historical situation out of which it comes and to which it was first spoken, because it speaks with spiritual directness a message for all in every age. This is God's word to you and me as well as to ancient Israel, waiting to be redeemed from a captivity which had both temporal and spiritual aspects (vs. 12-13).

Basic religious teachings of the text:

1. The refreshing power of God's word, which in its influence is like the refreshing rain in relation to seed and harvest (vs. 10, 11).

2. The gracious invitation and plea that men everywhere would seek the LORD now, while it is yet the day of salvation.

3. The exhortation to true repentance (vs. 7).

4. The assurance to the penitent of full and free forgiveness.

5. The transcendent greatness of God, and of His thoughts and ways, which are thoughts and ways of mercy and peace. See Jeremiah 29:11-13. Compare Ephesians 3:10, "the love of Christ which surpasses knowledge." See also Isaiah 57:15.

New Testament echoes of the text:

1. There is an exalted loftiness to the claim about "my word" (vs. 11) that is very similar to the claim of Jesus concerning his word: "Heaven and earth will pass away, but my words will not pass away" (Matthew 24:35).

2. The whole theme of gracious invitation is so completely in harmony with the whole tenor of the New Testament gospel that it could have been lifted bodily out of one of the Gospels or one of the Pauline Epistles.

Quinquagesima Sunday

TOPIC FOR THE DAY: "The Path of Suffering."

TEXT: Isaiah 53:1-7.

THEME: A Man of Sorrows!

Relation of the text to the topic:

There is no mistaking the distinctive character and message of Quinquagesima Sunday. Standing on the threshold of Lent, it introduces the theme of the suffering of Christ for our sins; or, as Bo Giertz says, the theme of "the conflict of Jesus with evil, and his suffering." On Quinquagesima Sunday our attention is riveted on Christ's commitment to suffering and death in order to carry out the will of God for our salvation. During the Sundays in Lent which follow, attention is centered more on the conflict with evil which was involved in the commitment to obedience to the will of God.

The theme for this Sunday is well stated in I Peter 3:18, "For Christ also died for sins once, the righteous for the unrighteous, that he might bring us to God." The theme for the next following Sundays is equally well stated in I John 3:8, "The reason the Son of God appeared was to destroy the works of the devil."

Our text, which the ELC lectionary includes as one of the lessons for Quinquagesima, is one of the servant-passages in Isaiah which has unmistakable reference to the Messiah as the suffering servant of the Lord. In so saying we do not deny the close association between Israel as God's servant and the Messiah, who shares with Israel this vocation, and who fulfils it in a way which Israel could never have done. The servant prophecies, as also the seed of Abraham prophecies, combine in a marvelous fashion the mission of Israel and the mission of Christ; so that much that is said of Israel from the ideal standpoint of her Divine vocation is clearly a prophetic type and a spiritual symbol of that which is supremely true of Jesus, the Messiah. In Isaiah 53, however, the type fades completely into the background. Here we see in almost New Testament clearness the personal servant, the Christ, who was to perform the unique work of an obedient, suffering servant of the Lord in behalf of his people. We must not forget, however, that in performing this work he fulfilled Israel's calling to be "a kingdom of priests" with a unique spiritual ministry to the nations (Exodus 19:6). We may preach from this text as Philip did: "beginning with this scripture he told him the good news of Jesus."

Basic religious teachings of the text:

1. The humiliation of the servant. Because of his humiliation, his humble origin and appearance, men despised and rejected him. In so doing they increased the humiliation. He was indeed a man of sorrows, and acquainted with grief.

2. The vicarious nature of the servant's suffering and sorrow. The keywords in verses 4-6 are the pronouns. The language is crystal clear. "He" suffered because of "our" iniquities, and for "our" peace. That could never be said of Israel. That could only be said of one who is without iniquity and without sin. That could be said of none other than the Messiah, Jesus Christ. This is, as Dummelow says, "A remarkable prophecy of Christ, himself sinless, suffering that men might be delivered from their sins and the penalty due to them."

3. The unusual statement, "the chastisement of our peace" (ASV), which seems to mean a chastisement that results in our peace, adds another facet to the concept of peace so often set forth in the Old Testament prophets. This phrase comes close to the New Testament concept of peace with God. The rendering in RSV, "the chastisement that made us whole," can be defended, but it does obscure the fact that the Hebrew word is *shalom,* which is the usual word for peace.

4. The definite recognition that in this suffering of the servant was involved an act of God. "It was the will of the LORD to bruise him" (vs. 10).

5. The meekness with which the servant suffered, like the meekness of a lamb; and yet, different, because the lamb does not know what is about to happen, and the servant did. Together with the passover lamb in Exodus 12 this reference to the lamb in Isaiah 53:7 is probably the background for John's dramatic announcement, "Behold, the Lamb of God!"

New Testament echoes of the text:

As might be expected there are frequent allusions to and quotations from this chapter in the New Testament.

1. It was from this chapter that the Ethiopian eunuch was reading and about whose meaning he inquired of Philip; giving Philip the opportunity to preach Jesus to him. Acts 8:26-35.

2. Verse 1 is quoted in John 12:37, 38, in explanation of the unbelief encountered by Jesus in his public ministry. Paul quotes a part of the verse in Romans 10:16 and makes the same application.

3. Passages such as Luke 18:31-33 and Mark 10:32-34, referring to the mocking and the shame that awaited Jesus at Jerusalem as accomplishing the things written through the prophets, may refer in the first instance to this prophecy from Isaiah 53.

4. When the prophet says that "we esteemed him not" (vs. 3), the thought is very similar to that of John when he says, "his own people received him not" (John 1:11).

5. The description of the servant as bearing our griefs and carrying our sorrows is quoted in Matthew 8:17 and applied to Jesus' ministry of healing: "He took our infirmities and bore our diseases."

6. The prophet says that the servant was judged by his generation as being justly smitten and afflicted of God, as if he himself had sinned. The same charge was made against Jesus (John 19:7). He was accused of blasphemy in claiming himself to be the Son of God, and as a blasphemer he was said to be worthy of death.

7. The teaching that he suffered "for our transgressions" and "for our iniquities" is echoed in many places in the New Testament. See Hebrews 9:28; I Peter 2:21; Romans 4:25; I Corinthians 15:3.

8. I Peter 2:24, 25, is parallel in thought to verses 5 and 6 of Isaiah 53, and quotes some of their language.

9. The statement concerning the servant that "he opened not his mouth" when oppressed corresponds exactly with the otherwise strange silence of Jesus when he was on trial before the high priest and the governor. He did not resist; he was obedient to the Father's will.

First Sunday in Lent

TOPIC FOR THE DAY: "Temptation."

TEXT: Isaiah 49:8-16.

THEME: "In the day of salvation I have helped you."

Relation of the text to the topic:

In order to understand the choice of text for this Sunday we need to remember how closely related temptation is to testing, and testing, in turn, to trials and affliction. In the Hebrew the verb which is translated "test" or "try" or "prove" is also translated "tempt." The verb is used with God as the subject, as when God tested or proved Abraham (Genesis 22:1); it is also used with Israel as the subject, as when they found fault with the Lord at Massah-Meribah (Exodus 17:7). We know that God never tempts anyone (James 1:13); but He does test them, both as to faith and obedience. The divine purpose with the "various trials" (I Peter 1:6) which His people experience may also vary. One purpose, for instance, might well be that of chastening. Another purpose is, as Peter also says, "that the genuineness of your faith, more precious than gold which though perishable is tested by fire, may redound to praise and glory and honor at the revelation of Jesus Christ" (I Peter 1:7).

The connection between temptation and testing is this, that the same experience in life may serve at the same time as a test of faith and obedience, and as a temptation to unbelief and disobedience. It all depends on the interpretation given to the experience. When we are chastened or afflicted, God would use the experience for the purpose of drawing us closer to Himself, in a deeper faith, and with a firmer dependence on Him as the source of our salvation and as the strength of our life. But the adversary, Satan, is also busy; and he would give to human suffering the same interpretation that he did to God's prohibition in the garden of Eden; he would tempt us to believe that God is not good, and that His Word cannot be trusted. Jesus was tempted by the devil to turn away from the path of redemptive suffering. At the same time the experience was a Divine test of his willingness to be obedient unto death.

Our Isaiah text does not speak directly of temptation; but it does speak of the trials of God's afflicted people, Israel. The Divine purpose with the captivity of Israel in Babylon was chastening because of sin. Though chastened they were still His people; but they were tempted to say in their affliction, "The Lord has forsaken me, my Lord has forgotten me" (vs. 14). Like Hebrews 4:15, 16, and I Corinthians 10:13, our text tells of the power that comes from God to overcome this temptation to unbelief. It gives assurance of the faithful love of God, whose compassion is greater than that of a mother for her infant son. He does not forget. He does not fail. He answers His servant and His people with help in a day of salvation. The quotation of verse 8 in the Old Epistle text, II Corinthians 6:1-10, is significant. The prophet addresses this word of the Lord first to the servant; but the same truth is then applied to the people, seemingly through the servant's activity in their behalf. Paul rightly applies it to the preaching of the gospel in the New

Testament day of grace. Our help in any time of need, whether of testing or of temptation, lies in the assurance that God will let Himself be found by those who seek Him; for it is still a day of salvation.

Basic religious teachings of the text:

1. God's promise to hear and to help in a day of salvation. The promise was for the Messianic servant; he experienced the truth of it "in the days of his flesh" (Hebrews 5:7, 8). The promise was also for God's covenant people of Israel; and they experienced its truth in the redemption from captivity in Babylon, when God had compassion upon His people and comforted them. The promise is also for those who seek eternal salvation through faith in Jesus Christ, for now is the day of salvation (II Corinthians 6:2).

2. The mercy and the compassion of God, which moves Him to comfort His people and to lead them in paths of safety and of abundant provision for their needs. The temporal aspect of the situation of the moment should not be ignored; but neither should we fail to see the spiritual overtones which foretell a redemptive experience far greater than from the Babylonian Captivity. All of the prophets are looking always towards the ultimate goal of God's covenant and of His redemptive activity, but they could not always distinguish the times and the seasons: hence the blended perspective of prophecy.

3. The covenant faithfulness of God, so much greater than the highest human illustration of faithful love, that of a mother for her suckling child, the son of her womb (vs. 15).

4. The declaration of God's attitude towards Zion (vs. 16). Its first reference is to Israel. That must not be left out in our use of the text even now. But it also has reference to the New Testament Zion, the Church of Jesus Christ, in which the stream of Israel's history as the covenant people of God was destined to merge.

New Testament echoes of the text:

1. The quotation of verse 8 in II Corinthians 6:2. It implies a fulfilment of the principle laid down in the prophetic word.

2. In verse 8 as in ch. 42:6 and 49:8 the servant is spoken of as "a covenant to the people." It implies that the Messiah is to be the mediator of a "new" covenant, in which the original covenant of blessing with Abraham should finally be fulfilled. If this interpretation be correct

the passage is intimately related to the whole New Testament concept of a new covenant.

3. The quotation in Luke 4:18 is from Isaiah 61:1, 2, but the same truth of release from bondage and imprisonment is seen in Isaiah 49:9, and elsewhere. The spiritual kernel of the prophecy is evident in the New Testament use of it.

4. The language of verse 10 is woven into the statement by John in Revelation 7:16, 17, concerning the white robed throng that has come out of the great tribulation. Either the redemption from Babylon, of which the prophet certainly speaks though his prophecy is not exhausted by it, may be regarded as foreshadowing the greater redemption experience to come with the coming of the Messiah: or it may be regarded as essentially one with it, and as a part of it. God worked out His redemptive plan and purpose in time, in which there are successive stages of development; but we must not forget the essential unity in the historically unfolding process of redemption. The prophets interpreted the present in the light of the covenant past; they also saw the significance of today in the light of God's tomorrow. They used mixed colors to give in words a picture of things near and distant, with both spiritual and temporal significance. A partial experience of the truth of verse 10 in the experience of God's mercy now on earth points forward to the perfect experience in heaven, or in the new heavens and the new earth.

Second Sunday in Lent

TOPIC FOR THE DAY: "Victorious Faith."

TEXT: Isaiah 35.

THEME: A highway for the redeemed.

Relation of the text to the topic:

The presence of Jesus among men, and his ministry of compassion and healing, caused many to believe on him. Whether faith was weak or strong, Jesus accepted it, and strengthened it; until it became that victorious faith of which John writes, "This is the victory that overcomes the world, our faith" (I John 5:4). Sometimes the faith was strong and persistent; as with the Canaanitish woman, who kept on pleading for help in the face of seeming rebuff. Sometimes it was a very humble, and a deeply grateful, faith; as of the sinful woman in the house of Simon the Pharisee. Sometimes the faith was feeble, and flickering, as if about to go out; such was the faith of the man who met Jesus at the foot of the Mount of Transfiguration.

Our text from Isaiah resembles this last incident in that it contains a strong encouragement to have faith in God (vs. 3, 4). It is an encouragement to God's people of old in a definite historical situation. Their own weakness and insufficiency makes them fearful. They lack the power to save themselves. God's messengers are sent to strengthen the fearful hearts and the weak hands with a "fear not" from God. The admonition not to fear is backed by the promise, "He will come and save you." Faith is directed to a highway for God's redeemed, the Holy Way, in which they may walk with safety and return to Zion. It is indeed a picture of "Zion's Happy Future." The "times-coloring" is that of a bygone age, and in part, of a bygone experience; and yet, the experience which came to them by faith, and which caused them to rejoice with singing over God's salvation, was simply a step on the way towards the full experience of salvation that belonged to the happy future of God's Zion. Once more we see a blended picture, according to the shortened perspective of prophecy which combines the near and the distant in one; we should have no difficulty in seeing that the promises given here apply in full to the consummation of God's covenant purpose with His people, and that as principles of Divine action they apply all along the way. It is God who creates the victorious faith in fearful human hearts, and He does it with promises of His salvation.

Our text is closely tied in with the Old Epistle for the day in that both speak of the way of the redeemed as being also a way of holiness. Victorious faith leads in the spiritual realm to sanctification.

Basic religious teachings of the text:

1. The coming of God with salvation as a strong encouragement to faith and courage.

2. The personal relationship with God, "our God," "your God," which was the basic spiritual factor in the covenant with Abraham: "I will be their God" (Genesis 17:8).

3. The joy that is associated with salvation; essentially the joy of

restored covenant fellowship and blessing, but pointing to the perfect joy of heaven.

4. The concept of redemption and the redeemed.

5. The way of holiness, a reminder of Israel's original calling to be a holy nation. The concept of holiness points to God's spiritual work with Israel as well as to His delivering them from an earthly captivity such as they experienced in Babylon. The goal of the covenant, a holy people, will be realized through God's coming to save them. That goal was partly realized when the Jews returned to their own land after the years of spiritual discipline in captivity. It could not be completely realized until the coming of the Messiah: "he will come and save you" found in him its final and complete fulfilment.

New Testament echoes of the text:

1. The statement in verse 2, "they shall see the glory of the LORD," is practically synonymous with the statement in Isaiah 40:5, "and the glory of the LORD shall be revealed, and all flesh shall see it together." The latter passage is quoted in Luke 3:3-6 with this slight difference in wording, "And all flesh shall see the salvation of God." The prophecy speaks of a revelation of the glory of God's salvation.

2. Hebrews 12:12 is a paraphrase of the prophet's words in Isaiah 35:3, applying them to a new but similar situation. So may we apply them in our preaching today.

3. Jesus' answer when John sent to ask of him, "Are you he who is to come, or shall we look for another?" was to tell John of the works which he (Jesus) did. They are described in terms that are reminiscent of both Isaiah 35: 5, 6, and Isaiah 61:1; see Matthew 11:4-5. Some items in the prophet's description are purely figurative. Others may be both literal and figurative in their intention. They illustrate the truth that the salvation of God makes all things new; they point in the same direction as Revelation 21:5: but the language and the thought of the prophecy is such as befits the Old Testament situation. It is worded in terms of the national experience of Israel. It has spiritual implications for the future of the kingdom of God.

4. The streams in the desert (vs. 6, 7) vividly suggest blessings of God in the form of a thirsty land refreshed by springs and streams of water. The land is represented as being recreated in a physical sense. But spiritual blessings attended when God redeemed the captivity of

His people; and in the long range view there may be a real connection between a prophecy like this and the invitation and promise of Jesus in John 7:37-39.

5. The thought-correspondence between the highway for the redeemed as a Holy Way and Paul's statement in I Thessalonians 4:7 that "God has not called us for uncleanness, but in holiness" is evident. Both reflect the basic requirement of the covenant, that God's people be holy unto the Lord their God. The same truth is stressed in I Peter 1:14-16.

Third Sunday in Lent

TOPIC FOR THE DAY: "The Scope and the Power of Evil."

TEXT: Isaiah 2:5-18.

THEME: Let us walk in the light of the Lord.

Relation of the text to the topic:

This is one Sunday for which it is not easy to select an appropriate text from the book of Isaiah. The reason for this difficulty is that the texts for the day seem less unified in theme than is usally the case. The Augustana lectionary suggests "The Parting" as such a theme; but it does not seem relevent to most of the texts. It is more helpful to see in the texts for this day a continuation of the general Lenten theme indicated earlier, "The conflict or battle of Jesus with evil." The power and the scope of evil is clearly seen in the Old Epistle text, where light is contrasted with darkness (Ephesians 5:1-9). The exhortation of Paul, "walk as children of light," coincides with that of the prophet, "let us walk in the light of the Lord" (vs. 5). The Old Gospel text also reveals the power of evil, as Jesus defends himself against the charge of being in league with Beelzebub, the prince of the demons (Luke 11:14-28).

Our text has this in common that it also speaks of the scope of evil in ancient Israel, where the majority chose to walk in the darkness rather than in the light. The specific evils mentioned by the prophet are three: idolatry, after the custom of their heathen neighbors; the materialism that so often accompanies an increase in riches; and militarism, or the placing of confidence for defense in horses and chariots rather than in

God. The spirit of pride, as motivating their wrong attitude towards God, is also stressed. The prophet predicts "a day of the Lord of hosts," when judgment shall be visited upon all that is proud and haughty, and the Lord alone shall be exalted. That is one phase of the ultimate victory over evil. The other, and the more relevant aspect as far as Christian preaching is concerned, is the invitation to walk in the light of God's revealed will; that is, in the light of that revelation of Himself and of His gracious covenant love which culminated in Christ, in whom we behold the glory of God as in the only begotten from the Father, "full of grace and truth." He who is willing to walk in that light of God shall have the victory over evil and over the evil one.

Basic religious teachings of the text:

1. The characteristic Isaianic emphasis on pride as a basic aspect of human sin.

2. The unholy trinity of idolatry, materialism, and militarism, as especially flagrant sins of the times, then and now.

3. The invitation to "the victorious life" in a willing walk in the light of God's revealed word.

4. The warning that there will come a day of judgment upon pride and upon every form of human sin and evil.

5. The prediction of a day of victory when the Lord, and He alone, shall be exalted.

New Testament echoes of the text:

1. "The light of the Lord" (vs. 5), expresses almost the identical truth as when John says, "God is light, and in him is no darkness at all" (I John 1:5).

2. The invitation to walk in the light has its parallels in the teaching of Jesus, of John, and of Paul.

3. There is a marked similarity of language between verse 10 (as well as verses 19-21) and Revelation 6:15-17. "The great day of their wrath" is essentially the same as "the day of the Lord of hosts," a day of judgment wrath and terror; except that the latter may be applied to any judgment of God in time, and not only to the final judgment. Judgment and redemption are the two principles of Divine action in relation to man and to human history; they move on like constantly repeated ocean waves towards a final climax and goal.

4. Paul as well as Isaiah speaks of the sin of self-exaltation against God, and wages spiritual warfare to destroy "every proud obstacle to the knowledge of God" and to take "every thought captive to obey Christ" (II Corinthians 10:5).

5. Verse 19 (which could have been included in our text) is reflected in the teaching of Haggai 2:6, which in turn is quoted in Hebrews 12:26.

Fourth Sunday in Lent

TOPIC FOR THE DAY: "Bread for the Hungry."

TEXT: Isaiah 52:7-10.

THEME: Good tidings of good!

Relation of the text to the topic:

The Eisenach Old Testament series includes our text as its selection for this Sunday. The Old Gospel text is the story of the feeding of the 5000 (John 6:1-15). Both the Augustana and the ELC lectionaries include two other texts from John 6, which interpret for us the sign which Jesus did in terms of its spiritual meaning. Jesus himself is the bread of life. The sign pointed to him, and to the words of eternal life that came from his lips, and to the gospel, which is the good news about him as the Saviour of the world. Man needs bread if he is to live here on earth; and yet, man does not live by bread alone, but by every word that proceeds out of the mouth of God (Deuteronomy 8:3; Matthew 4:4).

Our text from Isaiah also speaks of good tidings, tidings of peace, and of good, and of salvation. The LORD reigns! The LORD returns to Zion! The LORD has comforted His people! The LORD has redeemed Jerusalem! The LORD has made known His salvation to the ends of the earth! Such good news is like nourishing, strengthening, satisfying bread to the spirit of them to whom it is given. Israel experienced something of this joy of salvation in the return from Babylon; but that was only a prelude to the greater salvation to come. God, who knows the end from the beginning, gave a message to Israel by His prophet which had relevance for the immediate future, and at the same time pointed beyond it; for there is a finality about this salvation which certainly was not achieved in any return from earthly exile, even though this return did have real significance in relation to the final achievement of God's redemptive goal. Keeping the return from captivity in mind as the historical setting, when God returned to save His people whom He had afflicted because they had sinned against Him, we may without hesitation apply the prophecy as Paul does in Romans 10:15, to them who preach good tidings of salvation in any age and to every people, even the gospel of Jesus Christ. This is the true bread of life.

Basic religious teachings of the text:

1. The proclamation of salvation as good tidings, of peace and good.

2. The truth that "your God reigns." He reigns now; He has not abdicated from the throne of the universe which is His creation. He shall reign; for the day is coming when all men shall acknowledge that He is king, and shall submit themselves to Him and to His Christ.

3. The concept of a God who comforts and redeems His people.

4. The return of God to His people in renewed favor becomes to them the source of joy and singing, when all their wants are satisfied.

5. The universality of the salvation of God: all the ends of the earth have seen it, all the nations shall share in it, as the covenant of God with Abraham had promised.

New Testament echoes of the text:

1. Verse 7 is quoted in part by Paul in Romans 10:15.

2. The general relevancy of the prophecy for the Christian era and its resemblance to the Christian gospel has already been noted.

3. Verse 11, immediately following our text, is used in part by Paul in II Corinthians 6:17 as an admonition to the Corinthians to make a complete break with heathenism. The use indicates how spiritual principles involved in Old Testament prophecies may rightly be applied to new but similar situations. The prophet's Israel was to depart from Babylon, leaving its heathen uncleanness behind; so also the Gentiles in Paul's day must make a clean break with heathenism, and all its idolatries and immoralities, in order to be received into the Christian fellowship. God's people must be a consecrated people, a separated people.

That principle carries through from the call of Abraham to the Christian life today. It is not a matter of prediction so much as the application of fundamental spiritual truths to differing situations in the history of the kingdom of God. That is also the function of the preacher today.

Fourth Sunday in Lent

TOPIC FOR THE DAY: "Bread for the Hungry."

TEXT: Isaiah 41:17-20.

THEME: God will provide!

Relation of the text to the topic:

We list Isaiah 41:17-20 as an alternative text for this Sunday because it speaks of the gracious provision of God for the needs of His people, and therefore links up with the theme of "bread for the hungry," or of satisfaction for our deepest desires. The language is figurative. It suggests in the first instance the sort of provision that an Almighty Creator might make for a people returning from exile through an arid and barren desert to a neglected land that is itself like a wilderness. God will make all things new; He will make abundant provision for all their temporal needs. If as seems probable it had some reference to the return from Babylonian Captivity (as this whole section of the book of Isaiah does), it is quite evident that the hyperbolic language was not literally fulfilled at that time. We may well ask whether the choice of such language was not intended to be a sign in much the same sense as Jesus' miracle of feeding the 5000, pointing to the greater spiritual blessings of a right relationship with God now renewed, wherein they would experience all of the blessings of the covenant once forfeited by their own unfaithfulness. Such spiritual blessings attended the return from the Captivity; but as we have said before, the return from captivity was only a prelude to, and a prophecy of, a greater redemption that must come to pass before the consummation of all the blessings promised under the covenant could be realized. The prophets saw only in part, and they prophesied in part, and often their prophecy was colored by events which belong to the time of the end, or to the latter days, because they belong to "the times of restoration of all things" at which God's covenant purpose aims. It is not wrong to give a spiritual application to such a text as this, remembering always the historical milieu of the prophecy when first spoken.

Basic religious teachings of the text:

1. The Lord is mindful of the poor and needy, and will provide for their needs when they pray unto Him.

2. God will provide rivers of living water to quench the thirst of His people. There is a deep underlying unity between the teaching of this passage and of John 7:37-39. The Old Testament prophets never speak of temporal blessings as if they were an end in themselves; they are always associated with the spiritual blessings of the covenant.

3. The refrain from Exodus, and from Ezekiel, "and they shall know that I am the LORD," is pertinent here; for the purpose with the Divine promise of such abundant provision, and the purpose with the experience of His blessings by His people, is that they might learn to know Him and to acknowledge Him as the Giver of these good gifts and as their God.

Fifth Sunday in Lent

TOPIC FOR THE DAY: "Hatred Against Jesus Increasing. Jesus Condemned to Death."

TEXT: Isaiah 53:7-9.

THEME: The Lord's servant the victim of oppression and judgment.

Relation of the text to the topic:

Any portion of Isaiah 53 makes a suitable text for any Sunday in Lent. Its overall theme, "The suffering of the Lord's servant," is the overall theme of Lent. One suggestion for preaching from the old Testament would be to use the five paragraphs that make up this servant-prophecy (Isaiah 52:13—53:12) as lessons for the first five Sundays in Lent.

However, there are other texts that match the general topic for each Sunday even better than does Isaiah 53. The emphasis up to this point in Lent, with the exception of Quinquagesima Sunday, is more on Jesus' conflict with evil than on his own personal experience of suffering at the hands of evil men. The texts for the Fifth Sunday in Lent, however, focus attention on the rising hatred against Jesus, and on the plotting that led to his condemnation to death. That he suffered innocently, being wrongfully accused, is the clear testimony of the New Testament. Such is also the teaching of the prophet in our text, which in this case is selected from Isaiah 53.

Two words stand out in the text: oppression and judgment. From the human angle these were the cause of the death of the servant. We do not overlook the Divine angle, that it was also the will of the Lord to bruise him (vs. 10). Verse 9 makes even clearer this picture of a man who is innocent of violence and deceit, or of any sin, and yet is condemned to death, and in his death is "numbered with the transgressors" (vs. 12), and his grave made with the wicked (vs. 9). Verse 8 brings out the truth that he suffered vicariously, "for the transgression of my people," who were the really guilty ones and deserving of the judgment of death. Verse 7 overlaps our Quinquagesima text. A little repetition is a good thing.

Basic religious teachings of the text:

1. The natural enmity of men against God, and their spiritual blindness, which can cause them to condemn the innocent and to reject the One whom God has sent.

2. The innocent suffering of the servant, as the one oppressed and falsely judged by men.

3. The vicarious nature of the suffering and death of God's servant for God's people.

4. The willing obedience of the servant: the human oppression and injustice connected with the crucifixion did not obscure for Jesus the truth taught by the prophet, that it was the Father's will that he should suffer for the sins of the world.

New Testament echoes of the text:

1. The New Testament references to verse 7 are listed under Quinquagesima Sunday. So also are some of the references to the truth

that the servant suffered vicariously (vs. 8).

2. The death of Jesus between two robbers, and his burial in the grave of the rich Joseph of Arimathea (Matthew 27:57-60), is a literal fulfilment of verse 9.

3. I Peter 2:22 is a paraphrase of the last half of vs. 9. The whole paragraph, I Peter 2:19-25, points to Christ as our example in patience when "suffering unjustly."

Palm Sunday

TOPIC FOR THE DAY: "Jesus' Triumphal Entry into Jerusalem."

TEXT: Isaiah 45:21-25.

THEME: Every knee shall bow unto the Lord God, our Saviour.

Relation of the text to the topic:

In terms of the life of Jesus our Saviour the significant event connected with Palm Sunday is his triumphal entry into Jerusalem. For a few fleeting moments the people seemed ready to acknowledge him as the Messiah and to receive him as their king. The significance of that incident is shown by the evangelist to be threefold; 1st, that Jesus with design presented himself to them as Messiah and king, in literal fulfilment of the prophecy of Zechariah, "Fear not, daughter of Zion; behold, thy king is coming, sitting on an ass's colt" (John 12:15; Zechariah 9:9); 2nd, that the people acclaimed him as the Messianic king, crying out, "Hosanna! Blessed be he who comes in the name of the Lord, even the King of Israel" (John 12:13); and 3rd, that the disciples did not understand these things at first, but they remembered them when Jesus was glorified, and they associated the homage on Palm Sunday with that which belonged to him as the risen and ascended Lord.

The text selected for Palm Sunday is Isaiah 45:21-25. It does not speak directly of the Messiah, yet it has Messianic significance, as all Old Testament "theology" does; for the God revealed by the prophets is not only the God of Abraham but He is also the God and Father of our Lord Jesus Christ. The Incarnation is our key to many an Old

Testament passage (such as this one) which speaks of God as the only
Saviour. In the light of the Incarnation we can see that Isaiah 45:22 is
simply made more explicit by Acts 4:12; and that the language and
thought of Isaiah 45:23 is correctly applied in Philippians 2:9-11 to
Jesus Christ. Our text connects up with the Palm Sunday theme through
its marked similarity with the Old Epistle for the day, Philippians 2:5-
11; especially with that part of it which declares the exaltation of the
Christ as Lord, to which the triumphal entry also pointed. "To me every
knee shall bow," says the LORD, who is a righteous God and a Saviour,
to whom all the ends of the earth are admonished to look and be saved.
This God is the One who exalted Jesus and gave him the name above
every name, that "at the name of Jesus every knee should bow," and
that every tongue should confess that he is Lord, "to the glory of God
the Father."

Basic religious teachings of the text:

1. That the Lord (Jehovah) alone is God, and that there is no other
Saviour than this God who revealed Himself to Abraham, and continued
to reveal Himself in ever clearer words and works, until in the fulness
of time He was manifested "in human flesh" in the Person of Jesus
Christ, God's Son, our Lord.

2. That the day is surely coming when all men shall bow the knee
to the living God and Saviour, and shall swear by His name; a prophecy
which will be fulfilled when Jesus Christ is acknowledged as universal
Lord, and God the Father is glorified in him.

3. That in the Lord God alone are righteousness and strength to be
found, and to Him shall men come seeking righteousness, and in Him
shall all the seed of Israel triumph. As Delitzsch says in explanation of
Psalm 4:1, "O God of my right (ASV "righteousness"): "Jehovah is
the possessor of righteousness, the author of righteousness, and the
vindicator of misjudged and persecuted righteousness."

4. That God's enemies shall be put to shame, and that His people,
the seed of Israel, shall glory in Him.

New Testament echoes of the text:

1. Verse 23 is quoted by Paul in Romans 14:11, and the thought
expanded in Romans 14:9-12, with special reference to the final judgment: "for we shall all stand before the judgment seat of God."

2. The last line of verse 23 is incorporated in the Pauline statement in Philippians 2:10, with reference to the name of Jesus.

3. The concept of God as Saviour is common to the Old Testament and the New alike. See "God my Saviour," Luke 1:47, as an illustrative example.

Good Friday

TOPIC FOR THE DAY: "The Crucifixion."

TEXT: Isaiah 53:10-12.

THEME: The death of the Lord's servant.

Relation of the text to the topic:

Both the Augustana and the ELC lectionaries include the whole "Suffering Servant" passage, Isaiah 52:13—53:12, as the Epistle for Good Friday. It might indeed be well to read the whole passage, and perhaps to preach on it occasionally, so as to give the complete picture at once; but the preacher will soon discover that the section is much too rich in detail to permit adequate coverage in one sermon. The last paragraph makes an excellent Good Friday text by itself, for it speaks specifically of the servant's death.

There are difficulties both of translation and of exegesis in these three verses; but the meaning of verse 12 seems clear, and even such diverse translations as the American Standard, the American Jewish, the Revised Standard, the Douay Version, Moffatt's, and the American translation of Smith and Goodspeed, are in substantial agreement as to the essential thought, if not as to the exact words. The servant poured out his soul unto death. In dying he was reckoned with transgressors, as if he were one of them (Luke 22:37). Yet, his was a vicarious suffering, for he bore the sin of many. In his suffering he prayed for his persecutors, and made intercession for the transgressors. Therefore the Lord exalted him and gave him victory (see ch. 52:13), dividing him a portion with the great: as one whose influence over the hearts and lives of men shall not die. The victory of the servant over death is strongly implied though not clearly stated in the text. Whatever the obscurities of text and translation in verses 10 and 11, there should be no hesitation in saying with Dummelow about the passage as a whole, "The prophet here plainly teaches the atoning efficacy of the death of the Messiah, the accomplishment of His work through His sacrifice and His glorious after-life."

Basic religious teachings of the text:

The quotation from Dummelow given above is a sufficient summary of the teaching. For a more detailed exegesis of the whole chapter see a good commentary.

New Testament echoes of the text:

1. John 1:29 reflects the teaching of verse 10, "he makes himself an offering for sin" (a trespass-offering), as well as of verse 12, "he bore the sin of many."

2. Romans 5:18, 19, seems to contain essentially the same teaching as Isaiah 53:11, with reference to the justifying of many, or "making many to be accounted righteous."

3. "A portion with the great" (vs. 12) is in harmony with the exaltation of Jesus as set forth in Philippians 2:9-11.

4. The statement, "he poured out his soul to death" (vs. 12), is reminiscent of Jesus' words in Gethsemane, "My soul is very sorrowful, even to death" (Matthew 26:38).

5. Jesus quoted the statement, "and he was reckoned with transgressors," and claimed fulfilment of it in relation to himself (Luke 22:37).

6. The bearing of the sin of many is a truth that is repeated in many places in the New Testament.

7. The servant's intercession for the transgressors reminds us of the first Word on the Cross, "Father, forgive them; for they know not what they do" (Luke 23:34).

Easter Day

Topic for the Day: "The Resurrection of Jesus Christ."

Text: Isaiah 25:6-9.

Theme: Death is swallowed up in victory!

Relation of the text to the topic:

This text does not speak of the death or of the resurrection of the Messiah. It speaks in eschatological terms of a victory over death comparable to that of which we read in I Corinthians 15, the great resurrection chapter of the New Testament. Paul quotes the first line of Isaiah 25:8 in I Corinthians 15:54, "When the perishable puts on the imperishable, and the mortal puts on immortality, then shall come to pass the saying that is written: 'Death is swallowed up in victory.'"

The theme of both prophet and apostle is the victory of God's people rather than of God's servant, the Messiah, over death. The prophet proclaims that victory as an act of God, "He will swallow up death for ever." The apostle also proclaims it as an act of God, but he connects it with the Messiah, saying, "Thanks be to God, who gives us the victory through our Lord Jesus Christ." The prophet speaks of this victory in terms of a fulfilment of the old covenant: "This mountain" has the same meaning as "the mountain of the house of the Lord" in Isaiah 2:2, and is a symbol of the religion of Jehovah which had its spiritual center there; the promise of a "feast of fat things" is figurative language for the spiritual as well as the temporal blessings under the covenant of God with His people; these blessings are said to include "all peoples," for "the veil" that covered them, and that separated them for a time from the covenant people, is taken away; there shall be an end of death, and of earthly sorrows, and of reproach and persecution, through the salvation of God. The apostle speaks of essentially the same things in terms of the new covenant and of the finished work of Christ. Such is the manner of prophecy. It lets redemptive history clarify many details as to "how" these things shall be; but it focuses our eyes continually on a covenant goal of victory for God's people through the salvation of God; for which salvation they, and we, wait in hope: rejoicing in one aspect of salvation even now, for there is salvation in the forgiveness of sins, but earnestly hoping for it in that other sense of which also Paul speaks of it in Romans 8:23-25, the redemption of our body from death.

Considering all of the New Testament "echoes" of this prophecy, as well as the inseparable relationship between Christ's resurrection and our own, it should not be difficult to preach an Easter sermon on this text from Isaiah. The fulfilment of the prophecy is through Jesus Christ our Lord. The victory over death began with his victory. It is comforting to know on the basis of Old Testament and New Testament alike, that there shall be a day when death shall be no more, "for the Lord has spoken." "Therefore comfort one another with these words" (I Thessalonians 4:18). "Therefore, my beloved brethren, be steadfast, immovable, always abounding in the work of the Lord, knowing that in the Lord your labor is not in vain" (I Corinthians 15:58).

Basic religious teachings of the text:

1. The promise of future covenant blessings (vs. 6). The language is figurative. The blessings are all-inclusive. "Every spiritual blessing in Christ" (Ephesians 1:3) can be seen from redemptive history to be included.

2. The inclusion of all peoples in these future covenant blessings of God. Such was God's intention from the beginning; see the promise to Abraham, "In thee and in thy seed shall all the families of the earth be blessed." God "desires all men to be saved and to come to the knowledge of the truth" (I Timothy 2:4).

3. The breaking down, therefore, of "the dividing wall of hostility" (Ephesians 2:14 ff.) between Jew and Gentile, and the creation of "one new man," with one way of access to God the Father. "There is neither Jew nor Greek—for you are all one in Christ Jesus" (Galatians 3:28).

4. The comforting truth of an eventual victory by the power of God over death and all earthly sorrow.

5. The experience of rejoicing in the salvation and the covenant fellowship of God, now and forever.

New Testament echoes of the text:

1. "The veil" here spoken of seems to be the veil of ignorance that covered the Gentiles (see Ephesians 4:17, 18); "the veil" in II Corinthians 3:14-16 has reference to the Jews in Paul's day and in our own, whose minds are hardened so that they do not understand that the old covenant

has been fulfilled in Christ. To both the word applies, "But when a man turns to the Lord the veil is removed" (II Corinthians 3:16).

2. The first line of verse 8 is quoted by Paul in I Corinthians 15:54 as being fulfilled in the resurrection.

3. The second line in verse 8, the reference to the wiping away of tears from off all faces, is repeated in Revelation 7:17 and 21:4; not as a quotation, but as if an integral part of the New Testament message.

4. The reference to "reproach" (vs. 8) reminds of Matthew 5:11 and I Peter 4:14.

5. The whole concept of eventual victory over death, and of a lasting restoration of joy and happiness, as a fruit of God's salvation, is in harmony with the New Testament hope.

Easter Monday

TOPIC FOR THE DAY: "The Witnesses of the Resurrection."
TEXT: Isaiah 43:10-13.
THEME: You are my witnesses.

Relation of the text to the topic:

There is no direct prediction of the resurrection of Christ in the book of Isaiah. The exaltation of the servant, after his experience of humiliation and suffering and death, certainly implies a resurrection (Isaiah 52:13; 53:11, 12). When Jesus said that it was written in the Old Testament scriptures "that the Christ should suffer and on the third day rise from the dead" (Luke 24:46), we may be sure that he based his statement on something more than the letter; there were hidden depths to the Old Testament revelation whose significance did not become fully clear until interpreted by the Master Teacher or until exemplified in the life of the Messiah.

For instance, when Jesus sought Scriptural proof for the resurrection of the dead, he found it in Exodus 3:6, "I am the God of Abraham, and the God of Isaac, and the God of Jacob" (Matthew 22:32). In its historical context the statement was intended to encourage Moses' faith in God as the living God. It was a reminder to Moses that the God of his fathers was living still. It assured him that what God was about to do now was in line with what He had covenanted then with Abraham, and Isaac, and Jacob, that He would do to and through their seed. Its primary purpose was certainly not to teach the truth of the resurrection of the dead. Did Jesus, then, misunderstand and misinterpret it? No, for the truth of the living God implies also the truth of a living people; and the covenant with Abraham pointed to blessings which could neither be completely fulfilled nor exhausted here on earth. Jesus drew the correct inference from Exodus 3:6: if there is a living God, who enters into an everlasting covenant with men, it follows that His people with whom He enters into covenant must be a living people; for "He is not God of the dead, but of the living" (Matthew 22:32).

If this line of reasoning be correct in this instance (and we base it squarely on Jesus' own teaching), how much more must it not be true in respect to the Messiah, God's servant. The living God, who is the author of an eternal covenant, cannot bring that covenant to its consummation through a dead Christ. The living God implies a living Messiah; a Christ who could indeed suffer and die, and must so do, but who could give no victory of the sort visualized and promised under the covenant unless he rise again from the dead and live forever. That is why our text is an appropriate Easter text. It speaks of witnesses to the living God and Saviour, and to His mighty acts of salvation in those preparatory Old Testament days, which are so closely related historically and spiritually to that mightiest act of all when He raised Christ from the dead, and gave him glory (I Peter 1:21); "so that your faith and hope are in God." The transition from witnesses to a living God to witnesses to the living Christ is as natural and easy as is the transition from the theology of the Old Testament to that of the New, or from the God of Abraham, and of Isaac, and of Jacob, to the God and Father of our Lord Jesus Christ. "Because I live, you will live also," said Jesus (John 14:19); and in so saying he simply made explicit the truth that was implicit in the Old Testament theology of the living God.

Basic religious teachings of the text:

1. Its theology: I am the LORD (Jehovah), and I am God, and besides me there is no God and no saviour.

2. Its appeal to witnesses: "you are my witnesses"; witnesses of what I have done, and witnesses as to who I am; witnesses of God's redemptive works, and witnesses of His self-revelation to them under the covenant.

3. Its firm foundation of faith in the power of the living God to perform His purpose of salvation: "I work and who can hinder it?"

New Testament echoes of the text:

There is no direct trace of its teaching anywhere in the New Testament, but its theology is the same as that which is revealed in the Person and in the works of Jesus Christ. For that reason the resemblance between the twice-repeated "you are my witnesses" and the similar statement in Acts 1:8; "you shall be my witnesses," is not a surface one only. There is also a real resemblance in though between the question in verse 13, "I work and who can hinder it?", and the question of Paul in Romans 8:33, 34, "It is God who justifies; who is to condemn?" For "our God is in the heavens; he does whatever he pleases" (Psalm 115:3).

First Sunday After Easter

TOPIC FOR THE DAY: "The Lord Liveth."

TEXT: Isaiah 4:2-6.

THEME: Recorded for life!

Relation of the text to the topic:

The Easter theme of the living Christ, the Author of life (Acts 3:15), "the first and the last, who died and came to life" (Revelation 2:8), continues; but it combines with the theme of the believer's life in him. The Old Gospel ends with the so-called key-verses of the Gospel of John, "these (signs) are written that you may believe that Jesus is the Christ, the Son of God, and that believing you may have life in his name" (John 20:30, 31). Something of the same emphasis is seen in the Collect for the day.

The text that we have chosen is Isaiah 4:2-6. The reason for the choice is chiefly its reference to a holy remnant, which is further described as "everyone who has been recorded for life in Jerusalem." The Hebrew could be translated "written unto life" (see AJV and ASV mg.). Moffatt translates, "all who are entered in the book of Life." The picture in the prophecy is that of a remnant that has been purged and cleansed from its filth of sin, and that is now called holy; this remnant experiences, as it were, a rebirth and a renewal of life in fellowship with the covenant Lord, who creates a protective covering over His people and provides for them a refuge from storm and from rain. Much of the language is figurative. Much of it reflects the history of Israel, past and present; its calling to be a holy nation unto the Lord; its unfaithfulness and sinfulness; the necessity of a Divine purging; the promise of a purified remnant, that shall live before God in obedience and experience His protection and care. It visualizes, as almost every prophecy in the Old Testament does, a day when God shall have accomplished His covenant purpose with and for His people. Such prophecies were not exhausted by the history of Israel; unless indeed we profess to see no connection whatsoever between the Old Testament and the New, between Israel as God's people and the Christian Church.

The prophet indicates here a work which required more in order to accomplish it than the purging fires of persecution through which Israel so often passed. The prophecy does not focus our attention on a half-way stop, but on the final goal. Whatever the local "times-coloring" of the prophecy, it points beyond the purely national experiences of Israel to the spiritual experiences of the children of God. For God's people must first be cleansed, in order that they may be holy; and God's people are like a remnant whose names are written "unto life," or "among the living," and therefore "in heaven" (Luke 10:20). The Messiah may not be mentioned in the prophecy; some believe that he is (see the phrase, "the branch of the Lord"). But whether the work of cleansing be ascribed here to God or to the Messiah matters little; in the fulfilment the work of God may be the work of Christ. If we keep firmly in mind the basic truth that God's covenant and Israel's history are ever incomplete without Christ and the Christian Church, we can readily see the connection between the prophet's "recorded for life in Jerusalem" and the New Testament concept of "the Lamb's book of life" (see book of Revelation), or of "the assembly of the first-born who are enrolled in heaven" (Hebrews 12:23). The Lord lives; by faith we too may be written "unto life."

Basic religious teachings of the text:

1. "The branch of the Lord" may be a reference to the personal Messiah; see use of the Hebrew word "tsemach" in Jeremiah 23:5 and 33:15, and in Zechariah 3:8 and 6:12.

2. The concept of the remnant.

3. The character and status of the remnant as holy. Holy because separated, consecrated, cleansed. See original calling of Israel, Exodus 19:6. See also our calling, I Peter 1:13-16.

4. The destiny of God's people as "written unto life."

5. The means of cleansing, the "spirit of judgment" and the "spirit of burning." A work of God's Spirit seems to be indicated, a work of just judgment.

6. A new creation; a new beginning, and at the same time a consummation. A theophany: a symbol of God's presence and gracious protection; a revelation of what God's people shall experience.

New Testament echoes of the text:

1. The concept of a remnant of Israel is repeated by Paul in Romans 11:4, 5.

2. There is an evident spiritual unity between the prophet's words, "recorded for life in Jerusalem," and the more full developed New Testament doctrine: names "written in heaven" (Luke 10:20); the church "enrolled in heaven" (Hebrews 12:23); "the Lamb's book of life" (Revelation 21:27).

3. The whole picture of cleansing, including the reference to a "spirit of burning," bears a marked resemblance to the words of John in describing the baptism of Jesus as a baptism "with the Holy Spirit and with fire" (Matthew 3:11-12; Luke 3:16-17).

4. Revelation 7:16, "the sun shall not strike them, nor any scorching heat," may reflect Isaiah 4:6, as well as 49:10.

Second Sunday After Easter

Topic for the Day: "The Shepherd and the Sheep."
Text: Isaiah 40:9-11.
Theme: He will feed his flock like a shepherd.

Relation of the text to the topic:

The appropriateness of our choice of text for this Sunday is self-evident. All the lessons for the day center around the concept of the shepherd and the sheep. Some speak of Jesus as the good shepherd, and as the Shepherd and the Bishop, or Guardian, of our souls. The twenty-third psalm speaks of the Lord as "my shepherd." Some emphasize the work of the shepherd, and others the experience of the flock; but whatever the emphasis, these two belong together. Some refer to the chief shepherd, and also to those who are set as under-shepherds to tend the flock of God. Isaiah speaks of God as the shepherd; but what is said of God in verse 11 is a perfect portrait of Jesus as the good shepherd. This would make a good Advent text; for the good tidings of the coming of God with Almighty power and with tender compassion, to rule, and to feed, and to lead, and to carry His people, even if they were partially true of the redemption from Babylon, find their deepest and final fulfilment in Christ, who is Immanuel, God with us, and who as a spiritual shepherd performs this work of God.

Basic religious teachings of the text:

1. The proclamation of the good tidings that God is here to help His people: "Behold your God!" Behold, the Lord God comes with might."
2. The description of God in terms of mercy and might: as a mighty one, who comes to rule over His people, and in defence of His people, as their king; "like a shepherd," who feeds His flock and gently cares for each one in it.

New Testament echoes of the text:

1. The statement, "his reward is with him, and his recompense before him," is echoed in Revelation 22:12, "Behold, I am coming soon, bringing my recompense, to repay every one for what he has done."

2. The general correspondence already noted between this shepherd-picture and the concept of Jesus as the shepherd; though this New Testament concept may reflect prophecies in Jeremiah and in Ezekiel as well as in Isaiah that speak of God (or of His servant David) as shepherd of His people.

Third Sunday After Easter

TOPIC FOR THE DAY: "Homeward Bound!"

TEXT: Isaiah 30:18-21.

THEME: The bread of adversity and the water of affliction.

Relation of the text to the topic:

There is a two-fold connection between this text and the other lessons for the day.

The first point of contact is that they have as a common theme the present trials and tribulations of God's people. The prophet speaks of them as "the bread of adversity and the waters of affliction." The reference is to the experience of the people of Israel, and the transition from the first part of the chapter would seem to indicate that they have been afflicted for their sins. But whatever the reason for the affliction, its purpose is clear: it is a time of waiting for both God and His people; the Lord waits for the opportune time to be merciful and to intervene as a "God of justice" in behalf of His people, and they in turn wait for His salvation; and "blessed are all those who wait for him." Beyond the present tribulation lies a happier future. The day is coming when weeping shall be turned into joy. That experience can come to the whole people of God, or to the individual child of God, here on earth. It may be of such an experience that the prophet speaks, in terms of the history of Israel; but if so, it reveals the Divine way of working, and the experience of the earthly Israel becomes a prophecy of the experience of all the children of God. In the world they have tribulation; but they have also a living hope, which is not limited to this earth but is inclusive of the eternal joys of heaven. They know a God who is gracious, and who hears the cry of His people when they are afflicted;

they know the truth of the promise, "when he hears it [i. e. "your cry"], he will answer you."

But we must then be willing to keep His covenant and to walk in His ways, so that He can pour out His blessings upon us here on earth, and in heaven forever. The second point at which our text reflects the general theme for the day is in its reference to a way. "This is the way, walk in it" (vs. 21) was the word to Israel. "I am the way, and the truth, and the life: no one comes to the Father, but by me" (John 14: 6), is the word of Jesus to all mankind. There is a way that leads to a blessed goal of communion with God as a dear heavenly Father; but as with every way, it will not bring us to our goal unless we walk in it. In terms of God's way that means faith and obedience. The theme of "Homeward Bound" is most appropriate, for it suggests the thought of the joys of heaven while we walk in faith and obedience to God here on earth; and it helps us to understand "the chastening of the Lord" as a part of His loving purpose to help us to walk in the way and to reach the goal.

Another appropriate text for this Sunday is Isaiah 40:26-31, the Eisenach Old Testament selection, which we have used for the Fourth Sunday after Epiphany.

Basic religious teachings of the text:

1. The long-suffering of God who "waits to be gracious." God is gracious and merciful by nature; but He waits until such a time as we are ready, that He may prove Himself to be gracious and may have mercy upon us. He will be gracious when we sincerely pray for His grace and favor.

2. The right attitude of God's people in time of trial is also one of waiting. A right prayer is not demanding but pleading; it presents its needs to God, and then trustingly waits for Him.

3. For them who wait for God's help there will come a time when they shall weep no more; for they shall receive mercy, and shall find grace to help in time of need. It is an experience of the Christian here and now. It shall be his experience in heaven.

4. When God gives the bread of adversity and the waters of affliction, they accentuate rather than obscure the word of the spiritual teachers of His people, "This is the way, walk in it." Afflictions are intended to make us seek God more earnestly. We learn from them to stay close to

God in prayer, and to walk trustingly where He leads us. For our Teacher in all these things is none other than God, whose will for us is gracious and His way good.

New Testament echoes of the truth:

1. When II Peter 3:9, 15, speaks of the forbearance of God, which delays with judgment in the hope of salvation, it voices the same truth as when Isaiah 30:18 speaks of God's waiting that He may be gracious and merciful. When God afflicts His people it is for chastening rather than for destruction. God is ever slow to anger, and abounding in steadfast love and faithfulness (Exodus 34:6).

2. Each reference in Isaiah to the time when there shall be no more weeping seems to point to the ideal time of the end, and therefore to connect up with similar statements in the book of Revelation.

3. The promise to hear and to answer prayer is similar to every New Testament promise of answer to prayer; see Matthew 7:7-11.

4. The general parallelism between Isaiah's picture of adversity and affliction, to be followed by happiness under the renewed covenant blessings of God, and the New Testament picture of the Christian's life on earth as a time of tribulation, to be followed by the peace and joy and glory of heaven, has already been noted.

Fourth Sunday After Easter

TOPIC FOR THE DAY: "Sanctification in the Truth."

TEXT: Isaiah 65:13-16.

THEME: The God of truth.

Relation of the text to the topic:

There is no clearly discernible theme running through the lessons for the Fourth Sunday after Easter. The theme suggested in the Augustana lectionary, "The Blessing of Christ's Absence," harmonizes well with the teaching of the Old Gospel text, John 16:5-15, but it has no relation to some of the other texts.

An interesting point of unity between many of the texts is the word "truth." In the Old Epistle text we hear of "the word of truth" (James 1:18), "the implanted word, which is able to save your souls" (James 1:21). In the Old Gospel text Jesus speaks of the coming of "the Spirit of truth," who "will guide you into all the truth" (John 16:13). Another Gospel selection, from John 17:9-17, contains the well known words of Jesus, "Sanctify them in the truth; thy word is truth" (vs. 17). In another Epistle selection we are told how we may know that we are "of the truth" (I John 3:19).

In our text from Isaiah we hear of "the God of truth," by whom His servants shall bless themselves, and in whose fellowship "the former troubles are forgotten." The word truth in this verse is the Hebrew word Amen. It opens up the whole concept of a God who is faithful and true. As the God of truth in this sense of covenant faithfulness He will satisfy the desires of His servants and will make their hearts sing for joy. Standing in close proximity to the prophecy of "new heavens and a new earth" which follows, the prophecy seems to present in Old Testament language the same promise of joy in the Lord which is so prominent a part of our Christian faith and hope. It is a joy which is partly a present experience, but which belongs also, and perhaps preeminently, to the future. There is an eschatological aspect to many of these Isaiah prophecies that we must not miss in reading and in preaching. It should certainly not be difficult to connect "the God of truth" with "the word of truth." Nor should it be difficult to see how each is related to the same experience of joy in the Lord. Faith in "the God of Amen (truth)" blossomed in the fulness of time into faith in him who is called "Faithful and True" (Revelation 19:11), as well as "The Word of God" (Revelation 19:13) and "King of kings and Lord of lords" (Revelation 19:16).

Basic religious teachings of the text:

1. Most important, of course, is the concept of "the God of truth (or Amen)." It agrees with the revelation of the LORD (Jehovah) in Exodus 34:6, as a God "abounding in stedfast love and faithfulness." It suggests a covenant-making and covenant-keeping God, who can be trusted to "show faithfulness to Jacob, and stedfast love to Abraham" (Micah 7:20), which are essential characteristics of the covenant that He made with them, and with us who through faith in Jesus Christ are

also Abraham's seed (Galatians 3:29). Hesed and emeth, lovingkindness and truth (ASV), stedfast love and faithfulness (RSV), are the two most important words in the covenant theology of the Old Testament; and emeth and Amen come from the same root and have essentially the same religious significance. The emphasis is on faithfulness even when we translate as truth; a significant Old Testament contribution to the concept of truth.

2. The Hebrew word translated "bless himself" is the same word that is used in the covenant of blessing with Abraham: "in thee and in thy seed shall all the families of the earth be blessed" (ASV)—"by you and by your descendants shall all the families of the earth bless themselves" (RSV). The form of the verb in our text is the Hithpael, as in Genesis 22:18 and 26:4. The Hithpael is normally a reflexive, and is so translated in our text. In Genesis the Hithpael alternates with Niphal forms in chapter 12:3; 18:18; and 28:14. The Niphal may be reflexive, but it is also used regularly as a passive. In the original covenant promise to Abraham there may be room for both the passive and the reflexive significance. The passive, "shall be blessed," expresses the blessing as an act or as a gift of God, which it truly is. The reflexive, "shall bless themselves," is indicative of the attitude of faith which seeks a share in the blessing as something worthwhile. It is the latter which is evidently intended in our text. It is a prediction that "his servants" will truly acknowledge Him as their God according to His covenant with them, and will seek Him in life, and will worship Him as the God of truth, and will experience His blessing according to the covenant.

3. The promise of completely satisfied desires and of joy of heart for those whom God calls "my servants." Note the contrary picture of the rebellious, spoken of earlier in the chapter.

New Testament echoes of the text:

1. The contrasting picture of joy and sorrow in verses 13-14 corresponds exactly with the teaching of Jesus in Matthew 8:11-12 and elsewhere.

2. The use of the word "Amen" as if it were almost a personal name for God and as descriptive of His character is reflected in II Corinthians 1:20, and still more clearly in Revelation 3:14, where Jesus is called "the Amen, the faithful and true witness."

3. The general concept of God as faithful is found frequently in the

New Testament; see I Corinthians 1:9 and 10:13; II Corinthians 1:18; I Thessalonians 5:24. So is the concept of truth. See the significant statement in John 1:14, 17, concerning the Son, "full of grace and truth."

Fifth Sunday After Easter

TOPIC FOR THE DAY: "Prayer."
TEXT: Isaiah 56:6-8.
THEME: My house of prayer.

Relation of the text to the topic:

The Fifth Sunday after Easter is also known as "Prayer Sunday." The theme of prayer is evident in most of the lessons, from Jesus' teaching concerning prayer in his name to his own intercessory prayer for his disciples and his teaching of the disciples how to pray. Our text is most appropriate in that it speaks of God's house as a house of prayer. It is appropriate also because it predicts that "foreigners" shall join themselves to the Lord "to minister to him, to love the name of the Lord, and to be his servants"; so that God's house shall be "a house of prayer for all peoples."

The prophecy is spoken from the viewpoint of the covenant with Israel; but its emphasis on the universality of the covenant privileges points forward to the day of the new covenant and the conversion of the Gentiles, in fulfilment of the original covenant with Abraham that all the peoples of the earth should be blessed in his seed. It is therefore particularly appropriate as a text on this Sunday so near to Pentecost. Even though "my holy mountain" and "my house of prayer" refer in the first instance to the temple mount, and to the temple, the forward reference to the Christian era is not excluded. It contains a prediction, and it lays down a principle. What was true then is true now, that God's house is a house of prayer. It may also be a "meeting-house" (see Exodus 25:22) and a place of preaching, but it is preeminently a house of prayer. The burnt offerings and the sacrifices of the Old Testament temple have been replaced with the spiritual sacrifices of a broken spirit and of a contrite heart (Psalm 51:17), and with the praises of the forgiven sinner; but we do not forget that these were the very things which the Old Testament sacrifices symbolized as touching the worshipper in his relation to God. The difference between then and now lies chiefly in the greater freedom of access that is ours now in Christ. We may pray with even greater boldness than they, because Christ has opened a new and living way to the mercy-seat. (Hebrews 10:19-20). Let us not fail to use the privilege that is ours. Let us make our house of God a place of prayer as well as of preaching.

Incidentally, the Eisenach Old Testament selection for this Sunday is Isaiah 55:6-11, where the emphasis is on the Word of God. Isaiah 56:6-8 makes a better selection because of its emphasis on prayer in the house of God.

Basic religious teachings of the text:

1. The universality of the covenant, in that foreigners also are seen to be included.

2. The spiritual marks of the covenant: to serve the Lord (see Exodus 19:6; to love His name (Deuteronomy 6:4, 5): and to keep the covenant by obedience to that which is commanded. The reference to the sabbath is explained by Exodus 31:12-17. The sabbath was the outward sign of the covenant with Israel, just as circumcision was the sign of the covenant with Abraham.

3. The joyful aspect of worship; the privilege of prayer. That was true of worship in the Old Testament. Should it not be even more true of Christian worship? Is it always so?

4. The purpose with every earthly house of God is to be a house of prayer for all peoples. There must be no respect of persons, in the sense of discrimination against the poor (James 2:1 ff.). There must be no drawing of the color line, or of any other line that would exclude any "foreigner" from our houses of worship or from our Christian fellowship of prayer.

New Testament echoes of the text:

1. Romans 12:1, in speaking of the presenting of our bodies as a living sacrifice, in a spiritual worship, is not far removed from the spiritual emphasis of this text.

2. The key-clause, "My house shall be called a house of prayer for all peoples," was quoted by Jesus when he cleansed the temple of its

unspiritual commercialism; see Matthew 21:12-13; Mark 11:15-17; and Luke 19:45-46. It is combined with a quotation from Jeremiah 7:11, "You have made it a den of robbers." Matthew omits from the Isaiah quotation the phrase "for all peoples." Mark and Luke include it. Though that was not the point of emphasis with Jesus, whose concern at the moment was with the perversion of the spiritual function of the temple by the Jews, it definitely belongs in the picture.

3. The language and the thought of verse 8 is reflected in John 10: 16; it indicates the universal outlook of the prophecy, which has reference both to the lost sheep of the house of Israel and those other sheep of which Jesus spoke.

Ascension Day

Topic for the Day: "From Humiliation to Exaltation."

Text: Isaiah 52:13-15.

Theme: My servant shall be exalted.

Relation of the text to the topic:

There is only one text in the Old Testament that has direct reference to the exaltation of the Messiah to sit at the right hand of God, and that is Psalm 110. The exaltation of the servant in Isaiah 52:13 is a more general description, which in fulfilment may include both the resurrection and the ascension. Isaiah 52:13-15 makes a good text for Ascension day, for its theme is the same as the topic for the day indicated above, "from humiliation to exaltation."

Basic religious teachings of the text:

1. The humiliation of the servant, causing many to be astonished at him (vs. 14).

2. The exaltation of the servant of the Lord (vs. 13).

3. The effect upon the nations and their rulers (vs. 15). They are startled by what they see as by some new thing. They stop to consider what they have seen and heard. The interpretation of what they see follows in chapter 53.

New Testament echoes of the text:

1. Paul quotes the last half of verse 15 in Romans 15:21 in support of his ambition to preach the gospel in lands which had not yet heard it. The wording is slightly different. The situation to which Paul applies the word of the prophet is included in the prediction.

2. The humiliation-exaltation motif is in complete harmony with such New Testament passages as Philippians 2:5-11.

Ascension Day

Topic for the Day: "The Coronation of Jesus."

Text: Isaiah 33:17-24.

Theme: The king in his beauty!

Relation of the text to the topic:

It is a sad fact that Ascension Day is not as generally observed in the Church as it ought to be. One obvious reason is because it falls on a weekday rather than on a Sunday; but even so, it could as least receive "honorable mention" among the festival days of the Church. The Apostles' Creed rightly lists the Ascension among the important things in the life of Jesus Christ, our Lord.

The selection of a second text from Isaiah may serve to emphasize the importance of the day. Ascension day has been called the day of Christ's coronation. It witnesses to the truth that Jesus is Lord as well as Saviour: Jesus is king. The text from Isaiah witnesses in like manner to the truth that the LORD (Jehovah) is king (vs. 22); just as He is repeatedly said to be a Saviour, and the only Saviour (Isaiah 43:3, 11; 45:21; Hosea 13:4). The incarnation joins the two into one; for what is said of the Lord is true of Jesus, the Messiah, who is God's servant, and God's Son. The salvation of the Lord in terms of His covenant people Israel has both historical and spiritual relevancy for the salvation and reign of Jesus Christ, as preparing the way for it, and as one in spirit with it. The salvation of which Isaiah speaks is not only a deliverance from earthly enemies (vs. 18, 19), but from sickness and from sin (vs. 24). The gracious reign of the Lord as a lawgiver, and judge, and king, is described in terms of an ideal future, such as is naturally associated with the consummation of the covenant; and redemptive history makes it clear that this consummation is inseparable from Christ. "Jesus as king" does not contradict the word of the prophet, "The Lord is our king"; for he reigns as the Son of God, to whom all authority in heaven and on earth has been given. Ascension day is the day of his coronation. In him we truly see "the king in his beauty."

Basic religious teachings of the text:

1. Its theology: God as our judge, lawgiver, king, and saviour (vs. 22).

2. Its glorious promise to Zion: a quiet habitation, a place of peace and permanence (vs. 20). Zion in the spiritual sense of the city of God; not limited to the earthly Jerusalem.

3. Its prediction that the inhabitants of Zion shall be healed and forgiven: sin and sickness shall be no more (vs. 24). A spiritual concept, indicating the nature both of the Lord's salvation and of His reign.

New Testament echoes of the text:

1. James 4:14 echoes Isaiah 33:22 in referring to God as the only lawgiver and judge.

2. The concept of Jehovah as king and the concept of Messiah as king exist side by side in the Old Testament, and unite in the New Testament in the testimony that Jesus is king.

3. Forgiveness of sin was a real experience under the Old Covenant, which prepared the way for and anticipated the New Covenant in Christ. The statement in verse 24 has a sweeping breadth to it that is comparable to I John 1:7, 9.

Sixth Sunday After Easter

TOPIC FOR THE DAY: "Waiting for the Promise of the Father."

TEXT: Isaiah 32:12-20.

THEME: Until the Spirit is poured upon us from on high.

Relation of the text to the topic:

There are a good many Old Testament texts that speak about the Spirit of God in relation to God's people. There are several such texts in the book of Isaiah.

The one selected for this Sunday contains a prophecy directed to Jerusalem. It begins with a warning of coming desolation upon the city and the land (vs. 12-14). This desolation will continue "until the Spirit is poured upon us from on high" (vs. 15). Then the land will be transformed again into a fruitful field (vs. 15), and there will come a corresponding moral reformation (vs. 16). "This change alike in man and in nature is attributed to an outpouring of the divine and life-giving spirit" (Dummelow). The moral reformation is characterized by justice and by righteousness. The effect of the work of righteousness is peace (vs. 17). The peace is pictured 1st, in terms of man s inner spirit or frame of mind, as quietness and confidence, and 2nd, in terms of external conditions, as an abiding in a peaceful habitation, and in secure dwellings, and in quiet resting places (vs. 18). For this outpouring of the Spirit the people wait on the strength of the promise given.

Conceding that all this may have reference first to an experience in the national history of Israel as God's covenant people, the prophecy is nevertheless one of those comprehensive pictures of covenant consummation that transcends any such experience in Israel's history. Like so many others, it seems to be a prophecy in which the ultimate goal is united in one picture with that which is on the way to the goal. It would be incorrect to say that this prophecy is a direct prediction of Pentecost. It might rather be said to refer to an activity of God's Spirit in another situation which foreshadows Pentecost. It stresses the truth that righteousness and peace are fruits of the Holy Spirit, and that without righteousness there can be no peace. In its attitude of waiting for the Spirit to be poured out it is very similar to the attitude enjoined upon the disciples before Pentecost. Its description of the moral transformation wrought by the Spirit links it definitely with the New Testament teaching concerning the Holy Spirit as our Sanctifier.

Basic religious teachings of the text:

1. The transforming power of the Spirit of God as seen in land and people: the wilderness becomes a fruitful field, and in the fruitful field righteousness abides, when men become obedient unto God's Spirit and experience God's blessings.

2. Righteousness must precede peace. There is no peace for the wicked (Isaiah 57:21). There can be no peace among men where unrighteousness rules. Even in the individual experience of peace with God, justification (being reckoned righteous) precedes peace (Romans 5:1). For righteousness implies rightness, and that means first of all being right with God. Nothing else can be right until we are right with God. This is the work of God's Spirit.

3. The effect of righteousness is peace. It makes men peaceable and peace-loving, and it enables men to live without fear of one another, in a spirit of quiet confidence.

4. The expectation of a day when there shall truly be peace on earth, when the prospect so simply and beautifully described in verse 18 and in Micah 4:4 shall become actual and real. This expectation many of the prophets shared.

5. The beatitude in verse 20, so vividly descriptive of those who live in peace. The word translated "happy" can also be translated "blessed."

New Testament echoes of the text:

1. There is a real parallelism of thought between verse 17 and the definition of the kingdom of God in Romans 14:17 as "righteousness and peace and joy in the Holy Spirit."

2. There is also a marked similarity of thought and language between verse 17 and James 3:18. In both, righteousness and peace are seen to be closely related.

3. The seventh beatitude, "Blessed are the peacemakers, for they shall be called sons of God" (Matthew 5:9), is in perfect harmony with the "beatitude" in Isaiah 32:20 when seen in its context of peace based upon righteousness and expressed in quietness and trust.

Whitsunday

(Pentecost)

TOPIC FOR THE DAY: "The Gift of the Holy Spirit."
TEXT: Isaiah 44:1-8.
THEME: I will pour my Spirit upon your descendants.

Relation of the text to the topic:

There is a definite promise in this text that God will pour His Spirit upon His people and will bless them. In that respect it resembles Joel 2:28, 29, which Peter quoted in his sermon on Pentecost. In the final analysis both may point to that which took place on Pentecost, although the Isaiah text may have reference first to an intermediate experience which foreshadowed the day of Pentecost. It is directed to Israel, who is here called "my servant." The background of the covenant with Abraham, and with Israel, is evident. The historical situation is the imminent return from the Babylonian captivity (see chapters 40-48). In this situation the Lord speaks of Himself as "the King of Israel" and "his Redeemer" (vs. 6). He encourages His servant Israel (the nation is personified) by reminding him that he was chosen of God and made by Him into a nation, and that this same God will help him now. Not even the unfaithfulness of His people can hinder the faithful God from carrying through with His covenant until it is fulfilled.

The key to the text is the glorious promise in verses three and four. This promise resembles the lesson for last Sunday, in that it seems to speak of a physical transformation of the land which is accompanied by a spiritual and moral reformation. There can be no question but that an experience something like this took place when Israel returned from Babylon. There was at that time a renewal of covenant blessings, both temporal and spiritual. The parallelism between "my spirit" and "my blessing" is interesting. The reference seems to be to an activity of God's Spirit in bringing the people of Israel into a new experience of the spiritual blessings of the covenant promise to Abraham and to Abraham's seed. Verse five may indicate that as a result of the Spirit's activity there will be a reaffirmation by many in Israel of their allegiance to Jehovah, the God of their fathers, and to His holy covenant with them as a people; or, more probably, it indicates such a pledge of allegiance to Israel's God on the part of many among the Gentiles.

Admitting the partial fulfilment of this promise in the historical experience mentioned, we may still ask, Was God's covenant goal and purpose fully realized in the redemption of a remnant of His people from Babylon? It is obvious that it was not. We ask further, Will that goal ever be fully reached, and that purpose be fully achieved? Faith replies that it will. But prophetic faith was not always given to see the times and the seasons. The partial fulfilment of a prophecy that is experienced in the immediate future often points beyond itself to the perfect fulfilment that is promised. It is as Paul says in I Corinthians 13:9, 10: "For our knowledge is imperfect and our prophecy imperfect; but when the perfect comes, the imperfect will pass away." That is why we do not hesitate to see in our text a depth of covenant promise that only Pentecost could fulfill. But remember that the Pentecost experience was not so completely unique as to deny all earlier manifestation of the gracious work of the Spirit of God.

Basic religious teachings of the text:

1. The position of Israel as God's chosen servant, His covenant people, with a Divine mission and with promise of Divine blessings.

2. The freedom from fear that is based on God's promise to help.

3. The promise of the Spirit, and of spiritual and temporal blessings, because God is a covenant-keeping God. "My blessing" is reminiscent of the promise of blessing to Abraham and to his seed, and through them to the world.

4. The prediction that others besides Israel will join themselves to the Lord.

5. The exalted theology of verses 6-8: King, Redeemer, Revealer, Rock, Lord of hosts, God alone.

New Testament echoes of the text:

1. The promise in verse 3a, "I will pour water on the thirsty land, and streams on the dry ground," may be taken literally as referring to physical or material blessings. The language may also be figurative for

the spiritual blessings of the covenant, so that the first half of the verse stands in synonymous parallelism with the last half. If figurative, there is a marked resemblance to Jesus' words in John 7:37-39.

2. The promise, "I will pour my spirit upon your descendants, and my blessing on your offspring" (vs. 3b), seems to be related in thought and in language to Joel 2:28 ff., which in turn is applied in Acts 2 to the Pentecost experience.

3. "His Redeemer" as a designation of God is definitely related to the New Testament teaching concerning redemption through Christ, though Jesus is not actually called "Redeemer" in the Bible.

4. The declaration of God that "I am the first and I am the last" (vs. 6) is in the New Testament applied to Jesus. See Revelation 1:8, 17, and 22:13.

5. God as the Rock may be related to Christ as the foundation (I Corinthians 3:11) and the chief cornerstone (Ephesians 2:20). See also I Corinthians 10:4 for another aspect of the spiritual symbolism of the rock. Christian hymnody has not hesitated to speak of Christ as the Rock on which we stand. It implies stability and security.

Whitmonday

Topic for the Day: "The Progress of the Spirit."

Text: Isaiah 11:10-16.

Theme: An ensign for the nations!

Relation of the text to the topic:

Among the texts for Whitmonday is one of the most beloved passages in the Bible, John 3:16. We may wonder at its assignment to this obscure and seldom celebrated day in the church calendar, but we can readily see the significance of the selection. Though it does not make mention of the Holy Spirit, it is a true Pentecost text; for the Holy Spirit's ministry is that of glorifying Jesus Christ the Son and of bringing all men to faith in him as their Saviour. Even at Pentecost Jesus Christ should be the center of our preaching. And the preaching should present him as "the Saviour of the world" (John 4:42). "For God so loved the world," says the little Bible (John 3:16); and other texts for Whitmonday stress the progress of the gospel, which is the progress of the Spirit, among the Gentiles. The message of Pentecost is inseparable from the message of missions; for we cannot separate the gospel of Christ from the love of God, and God would have all men to be saved and come to the knowledge of the truth (I Timothy 2:3, 4).

Such is also the message of our text from Isaiah. It is a part of a Messianic chapter, where attention is directed first to him who is called "the root of Jesse," upon whom rests the Spirit of the Lord; whose guiding motive is the fear of the Lord, whose judgment is in righteousness, whose every action is characterized by righteousness and faithfulness, and whose righteous reign is a reign of peace. In our text the root of Jesse is called "an ensign for the nations." Verse 10 is a prediction that the Gentiles shall seek him. Verses 11-16 are a prediction that the Lord will recover "the remnant of his people" and will gather together "the outcasts of Israel" and "the dispersed of Judah." The total picture is that of a salvation which includes both Jew and Gentile, and which is based on a true knowledge of God (vs. 9).

Shall we not say that this began to be fulfilled in the ministry of Christ, and continues to be accomplished by the ministry of the Holy Spirit, who now through the Church glorifies Christ as Saviour to Jew and Gentile alike. The fulfilment reveals a much deeper spiritual aspect to this ministry of the Messiah than does the prediction, for the fulfilment is often greater than the prediction. There are details in the prophecy that may apply to Israel primarily in a national sense; but the heart of the prophecy is the coming of a day when all men shall seek the Lord, and shall know the Lord, and shall live in the fellowship of His covenant and His people: and this heart of the prophecy is being fulfilled in Christ and in the ministry of the gospel. It is being fulfilled by the Holy Spirit, who through the preaching of the gospel is drawing all men unto Christ and preparing the way for his righteous reign of peace.

Basic religious teachings of the text:

1. The root of Jesse as a designation for the Messiah. It points to him as the son of David and as a righteous ruler or king.

2. The nations seeking unto the root of Jesse, who is the Messiah,

and unto the LORD (Jehovah). It points to the conversion of the Gentiles.

3. The recovery of the outcasts of Israel, God's covenant people, from dispersion. It points to the return from earthly exile and captivity (from Assyria, vs. 16), but it points also to a spiritual return into renewed covenant fellowship with God.

4. The highway for the remnant of God's people. It is a concept which has both temporal and spiritual significance. See Isaiah 35:8, "the Holy Way." See the reference to "the Way" in the book of Acts.

New Testament echoes of the text:

1. Verse 10 is quoted by Paul in Romans 15:12 as being fulfilled in Christ's relation to the Gentiles, who because of Christ "glorify God for his mercy."

2. "The ensign" in verse 10 serves as a rallying-point for the nations, and as a symbol of allegiance. We are reminded of the Christ lifted up (see John 3:14, 15, and 12:32), who draws men unto himself.

3. The seeking of the nations, or the conversion of the Gentiles, is reflected in many places in the New Testament.

Trinity Sunday

TOPIC FOR THE DAY: "The Spirit and the New Life."

TEXT: Isaiah 6:1-8.

THEME: Holy, holy, holy is the Lord of hosts! (or My eyes have seen the King, the Lord of hosts.)

Relation of the text to the topic:

Our text is the Eisenach Old Testament selection for Trinity Sunday. It has several significant points of contact with other lessons for the day.

In common with the Old Epistle text, Romans 11:33-36, it gives us a vivid picture of the glory of God, the Lord of hosts. Neither text refers directly to the doctrine of the Trinity; but since God is Triune, the glory that is revealed is the glory of the Triune God whether the truth that He is Triune be stated or not. One interpretation of the

Trisagion (Holy, holy, holy) is that it reflects the knowledge of the seraphim, who are always in the presence of God, that He is Triune.

In common with the Old Gospel text, John 3:1-15, it stresses the necessity and the possibility of a spiritual experience which we may well call a *new life*. The Isaiah text speaks of it as being essentially an experience of the forgiveness of sin; the Gospel speaks of it as an experience of being "born anew" and of having "eternal life." Luther's words in the Catechism may serve to connect, and indeed to equate, the two: "for where there is remission of sins, there is also life and salvation." The Isaiah text moves within the milieu of the Old Testament: the cleansing is brought about by a live coal taken with the tongs from off the altar and accompanied by the word of absolution. The Gospel text is clearer: the new life is the result of the ministry of the Holy Spirit, and of the Son; for eternal life comes through faith in the crucified Christ. In both instances, however, it is an act of God, and in it the glory of God's grace is revealed.

The same concepts of the forgiveness of sin and of cleansing are prominent in other lessons for Trinity Sunday. So also is the concept of fruit-bearing and of spiritual service as a result of the experience of forgiveness and of the new life relationship with God. In Isaiah's case it is expressed in his response to God's call for volunteers (vs. 8), and in God's command, "Go, and say" (vs. 9). In John 15:1-9 Jesus calls himself "the true vine" and refers to his disciples as "branches," which are cleansed by the husbandman in order that they might bear "more fruit." In Matthew 28:18-20 we have the Great Commission to go and make disciples. With these points of contact, Isaiah 6:1-8 makes an excellent Old Testament text for Trinity Sunday.

Basic religious teachings of the text:

1. Its theology: a theophany, in which is revealed the holiness, the glory, and the wonderful grace of God.

2. Its confession of sin: in the presence of the holy God Isaiah is convicted of sin in himself and in his people, and confesses his unworthiness to be in that holy presence.

3. Its pronouncement of absolution: the penitent, who confessed his sin and acknowledged himself to be worthy of condemnation, experiences the forgiveness of his sins and cleansing from his iniquity.

4. Its call for volunteers in God's service: the forgiven sinner hears and heeds the call and offers himself in holy service for God.

5. Its courageous faith: being forgiven Isaiah could say, "Here I am! Send me."

New Testament echoes of the text:

1. John 12:41 is a direct reference to the experience of this chapter and to the statement that "I saw the Lord." "Isaiah said this because he saw his glory and spoke of him."

2. In the book of Revelation we have similar pictures of God sitting upon a throne, high and lifted up; see Revelation 4:2, 3, and 20:11.

3. The description of the four living creatures in Revelation 4:8 is similar to that of the seraphim in Isaiah 6:2. Their songs of praise are almost identical.

4. The words of John in I John 1:7 are reminiscent of the words of absolution spoken to Isaiah (vs. 7).

5. There is a marked similarity between the experience of Isaiah and of Paul: when forgiven, they were ready to accept the call to serve; they were not disobedient to the heavenly vision (Acts 26:19).

6. The holiness of God is a basic New Testament concept. Jesus addressed God as "Holy Father" (John 17:11).

7. Verses 9-10 should perhaps have been included in our text, as they are closely related to it. There are many references in the New Testament to the truth enunciated in these verses; see marginal reference column in your Bible. For a very good discussion of the meaning of the verses see Chapter IV of G. A. Smith's Commentary on Isaiah.

Trinity Sunday

TOPIC FOR THE DAY: "The Triune God."

TEXT: Isaiah 63:7-16.

THEME: The covenant God of Israel.

Relation of the text to the topic:

The Augustana and the ELC lectionaries include Matthew 28:18-20 as the third Gospel for Trinity Sunday. It is in this text that we have the clearest reference to the Holy Trinity, Father, Son and Holy Spirit. It would seem that Trinity Sunday is an appropriate time for us to consider this fundamental Christian doctrine, that God is One and yet Triune. It is a doctrine which is not clearly taught in the Old Testament, for the needed emphasis then was on the truth that God is One (Deuteronomy 6:4, 5). There is a progressiveness, or a forward movement, in God's self-revelation which did not reach its climax until the Incarnation: when God in the fulness of time "sent forth His Son, born of a woman" (Galatians 4:4), it became clear that God is Triune as well as One, and some of the Old Testament foreshadowings of that truth took on a deeper meaning.

For example, in Isaiah 63 there is reference to God as our Father, and to the angel of His presence, and to His holy Spirit. The reference to God as our Father (vs. 16) is in line with the covenant concept of Israel as God's people and as God's children. Even in Exodus 4:22 we have the statement, "Thus says the Lord, Israel is my first-born son." That relationship was basic to the covenant, and references to Israel's position as a son or a child of God are not infrequent; but Isaiah 63:16 is one of the few passages in the Old Testament where God is addressed as Father. It is for that reason a truly remarkable passage as teaching in some sense the Fatherhood of God. However, it does not teach as the New Testament does that He is "the God and Father of our Lord Jesus Christ" (II Corinthians 1:3). It teaches as Jesus did in the Lord's Prayer that He is *our* Father; He is the Father of His people under the spiritual terms of the covenant. The New Testament makes clear the connection between the two concepts, God as Father in the ontological sense, and God as Father in the soteriological sense of the covenant; the Old Testament does not. We can only say that the truth of God as Father in the full New Testament sense is foreshadowed in the Old Testament, including the book of Isaiah.

So also with the "angel of His presence" in relation to Jesus Christ, the Son of God. The allusion is to the wonderful theophany in the time of the Exodus (Exodus 20:20-23 and 33:14, 15; Deuteronomy 4:37). It was God who was present with His people, and who saved them, and redeemed them, and carried them; but He did all this through "the angel of His presence": through the angel He revealed His presence and redeemed His people. We call this a theophany. There are many theophanies recorded in the Old Testament; but among them there is one, "the angel of the Lord," or "the angel of His presence," that seems to possess both a more personal and a more permanent character than the others. Some exegetes suppose this angel to have been an actual Old Testament manifestation of the Second Person in the Trinity. The theophany does foreshadow the truth of God's presence as seen in the greater theophany of the Incarnation (see Art. "Theophany," Westminster Dictionary of the Bible); but it does not predict it or teach it in direct language. We can only say that the truth that Christ is the Son of God and the living expression of His presence is foreshadowed in the Old Testament, and in this chapter of the book of Isaiah.

The same is true of the reference to the Spirit of the Lord as "His holy Spirit." This is one of two Old Testament passages where the Spirit of God is referred to as God's "holy Spirit": see Psalm 51:11. The adjective "holy" is not capitalized as in the New Testament. In fact, in Hebrew it is not an adjective at all, but a modifying noun; the literal translation would be "the Spirit of His holiness." Doubtless in the light of later revelation this is the Holy Spirit; but the Old Testament manner of reference is still that of God's Spirit as something belonging to God in much the same way as man's spirit may be said to belong to man. There is nothing as yet to indicate that the Spirit is a Person in the Trinitarian sense. All that we can say is that the truth of the Holy Spirit as one of the three Persons in the Godhead is foreshadowed by what is said here as well as elsewhere in the Old Testament. The New Testament uses some of the very words of Isaiah 63 in teaching us a right attitude towards the Holy Spirit. Therefore we do not hestitate to say that our text is a good Trinity text, because it does foreshadow that full truth concerning God which was clearly revealed when God sent His Son to be the Saviour of the world, and when the Son spoke of the coming of the Holy Spirit in that personal sense in which the Church has experienced His presence ever since (John 16:13-15).

Basic religious teachings of the text:

1. The steadfast love, goodness, and mercy of God, in faithfulness to the covenent with His people (vs. 7).

2. The personal relationship between God and Israel as His people, His children (vs. 8), whose Saviour He was.

3. The love and pity (compassion) of God as seen in the Exodus, when He saved, redeemed, and carried His people "on eagles' wings" and

brought them into covenant fellowship with Himself (Exodus 19:4-6).

4. The covenant promise of the presence of God as illustrated in "the angel of His presence" (vs. 9).

5. The rebellion of His people against "His holy Spirit," which constrained God to chastise them as if they were His enemy instead of His son.

6. The result of this chastening, as seen in vs. 11-14. We follow the translation of the Swedish version as well as of the American Jewish version in the first line of vs. 11: "Then His people remembered the days of old, the days of Moses, saying, Where is he—." In their affliction the ancient mercies of the Lord are called to mind. (RSV makes God the subject, the one who remembers. It is true, of course, both ways).

7. The prayer of God's afflicted people, who now seek Him in their distress (vs. 15); calling to mind His holiness and His glory, His zeal and His mighty acts, His former compassion.

8. The faith of verse 16. "The patriarchs might disown their descendants, but Jehovah's love is sure" (Dummelow). For similar assurance from God's side see Isaiah 49:15.

New Testament echoes of the text:

1. The concept of God as being rich in steadfast love and in mercy is reflected in many places in the Epistle to the Ephesians; see ch. 1:7 and 2:4.

2. "The angel of His presence" links the prophecy with the earlier covenant promise of God's presence with His people as their God. The theophanies, the spiritual symbolism of the tabernacle, as well as the prophecy of Immanuel, all pointed forward to the full realization of the truth of this promise in Christ.

3. Paul's admonition in Ephesians 4:30, "And do not grieve the Holy Spirit of God," reflects the declaration in Isaiah 63:10, "But they rebelled and grieved His holy Spirit."

4. The concept of the Fatherhood of God in relation to those who are called His people and His children under the terms of the covenant is prominent also in the New Testament.

First Sunday After Trinity

TOPIC FOR THE DAY: "Priceless Values."

TEXT: Isaiah 33:1-6.

THEME: The fear of the Lord is our treasure.

Relation of the text to the topic:

The theme for the day is set by the parable of the rich man and Lazarus (Luke 16:19-31). Lazarus sought and received treasures in heaven, whereas the rich man sought and received all his good things in his lifetime on earth. The same contrast is seen in the parable of the rich fool, who laid up treasures for himself but was not rich toward God (Luke 12:13-21), and in the teaching of Jesus concerning disciple-ship (Matthew 16:24-27). The prayer in the first Collect in the ELC lectionary points up the lesson for the day in these words, "that we may not, like the rich man, hear Thy word in vain, and become so devoted to things temporal as to forget things eternal."

At first glance our text from Isaiah does not seem to fit this theme at all. It speaks very definitely of things temporal: of the destruction of the treacherous enemy, meaning Assyria; of the deliverance of God's people Israel from the power of the enemy by the might of God's arm; and of a seemingly temporary stability ("the stability of your times"). But note that though these are temporal in character they are represented as being God's good gifts to His people. It is one thing to seek things temporal to the exclusion of things eternal, and quite another to recog-nize that we do often experience the blessings of "the Eternal" (Moffatt's usual rendering for the name Jehovah) here on earth. The important thing is to live in sincere covenant fellowship with God. Jesus said, "Seek first his kingdom and his righteousness"; but then he went on to say, "and all these things shall be yours as well" (Matthew 6:33). "These things" were the temporal things of which He had just been speaking. It is essentially a matter of putting first things first. The prayer in verse two of our text is a beautiful spiritual prayer, even if "our salvation in the time of trouble" may have reference to temporal as well as spiritual need; it reveals a priceless value in its attitude of trust in a gracious God and of waiting for Him "every morning." The statement in verse five that the Lord will fill Zion "with justice and righteousness" certainly points to priceless values; for "righteousness exalts a nation" (Proverbs 14:34), and it is also the "peaceful fruit" yielded by the Divine chastening in the life of His people (Hebrews 12:11).

"The fear of the Lord" is also a treasure, and is so called in verse six. It matters little whether we translate "your treasure" or "his treasure" (the pronominal suffix in Hebrew indicates the latter); for in the latter case the emphasis is on the value of this attitude of filial fear in the sight of God, which implies its value in the life of the people; and in the former case the emphasis is on its value for us because God regards it with favor and blesses it in our life-experience. "The fear of the Lord is the beginning of wisdom" (Proverbs 9:10). It is said of the Messiah that "His delight shall be in the fear of the Lord" (Isaiah 11:3). The fear of the Lord is that right attitude which was found in Lazarus but not in the rich man. It is of priceless value because it enables us to live aright here on earth, in fellowship with God by faith, and to learn from every experience of life, be it bitter or sweet, to put our trust in God. It is of priceless value because it leads us to seek first God's kingdom and righteousness. The fear of the Lord will move us to set our minds on things that are above rather than on things that are upon the earth (Colossians 3:2). It is of priceless value because it leads to inward peace, and, if many share in the fear, to outward peace as well. The surest way to stability in our times is through the teaching and the learning of the fear of the Lord on the part of all men.

Basic religious teachings of the text:

1. "Whatever a man sows, that he will also reap" (Galatians 6:7) applies to nations also (vs. 1).

2. Our help as individuals and as a nation is in the willingness of the Lord to be gracious to us in answer to our prayer (vs. 2).

3. God is exalted in the destruction of evil and in the overthrow of evil men, as well as in the victory of justice and righteousness among His people (vs. 3-5).

4. "The fear of the Lord is the beginning of wisdom," and therefore it is a true treasure (vs. 6).

New Testament echoes of the text:

1. Isaiah 33:1, Matthew 7:2, and Galatians 6:7 teach the same truth: "the measure you give will be the measure you get."

2. The teaching of Isaiah 33:6 is essentially the same as in Matthew 6:33. The fear of the Lord prompts us to seek first the things of God; then the experience of temporal blessings follows. Even when the temporal gifts are withheld, as they sometimes are for a season, the fear of the Lord brings its own reward.

Second Sunday After Trinity

TOPIC FOR THE DAY: "The Call to the Kingdom of God."

TEXT: Isaiah 1:2-4.

THEME: Rebellious children.

Relation of the text to the topic:

There is only one direct reference to the kingdom of God in the lessons for the day, and that is in Luke 9:62, "No one who puts his hand to the plow and looks back is fit for the kingdom of God." The call to Christian discipleship, as well as to fellowship, is prominent in all the lessons, however; and such a call implies the concept of the kingdom of God. In most of the lessons it is implied, if not clearly stated, that the call is rejected by many. In the parable of the great supper (Luke 14:16-24) the invited guests offer excuses. According to Jesus' teaching in Luke 14:24-35 the cost of discipleship is great: but unless we are willing to bear the cross, we cannot be disciples. The incidents in Luke 9:51-62 reveal how few were ready to surrender all and follow Jesus. The Epistle text from Hosea 11:1-7, included in the Augustana lectionary, tells of the disappointed love of God because Israel, His son, was bent on backsliding from Him.

This last text, itself from an Old Testament prophet who was a contemporary of Isaiah, is very similar to the one we have chosen from Isaiah 1:2-4. There is the same concept of Israel as the children of God, called by Him into covenant relationship with Himself, and taught by Him as a father would teach his children what that covenant relationship involved in the way of privilege and of duty. There is a sense in which the covenant can be equated with the kingdom of God: they are overlapping, if not completely identical, concepts; and the call of Israel into covenant fellowship was the call into the kingdom of God. But they rebelled against the Lord. That was the tragedy of the situation as the prophet describes it. Instead of accepting the call in its full spiritual significance they chose the life of sin, and of iniquity, and of evil-doing; they forsook the Lord, and despised the Holy One of Israel; they were estranged from the covenant and from the kingdom in its true spiritual sense. Men often act in the same way today. The call is spurned by those who have already been the objects of God's love; and it grieves God's heart. We can use this text to press the call into covenant with God today, and at the same time point out the tragedy of rebellion, and of rejecting the love of God.

Basic religious teachings of the text:

1. The covenant relationship: Israel called "my people" and described as children brought up by God.

2. The fatherly love of God as seen in His relation to Israel; the same tender attitude as in Hosea 11:1-4.

3. The rebellion of children against Divine love; against a God and Father *who is love* in all His dealings with His children. It shows base ingratitude. It shows also that they are less intelligent in their actions than animals, who know what is good for them.

4. The sevenfold description of their wrong attitude towards God and towards the covenant (vs. 4). A cumulative picture of their sinfulness, and of their apostasy from God.

New Testament echoes of the text:

There is no quotation from the text, nor is there any direct reference to it, in the New Testament. The basic religious teachings are the same, however.

Third Sunday After Trinity

TOPIC FOR THE DAY: "The Prevenient Grace of God."

TEXT: Isaiah 44:21-23.

THEME: I have blotted out your transgressions and your sins.

Relation of the text to the topic:

"The prevenient grace of God" is a theme that unmistakably fits the lessons for this Sunday. Among them are the parables of the lost sheep, the lost coin, and the prodigal son; the story of Jesus' calling of Matthew, and of His eating with publicans and sinners; and the significant teaching of Paul in Ephesians 2:1-10, where salvation is shown to be a gift of God. Instead of "prevenient" we might simply say "forgiving" grace; although the emphasis throughout is twofold, 1st, that God takes the initiative in grace, and 2nd, that His grace is expressed in forgiveness and salvation. The response of the sinner to the grace of God in penitence and faith is also clearly taught; but the chief emphasis is on God's saving grace.

There are several texts in the book of Isaiah that speak in similar fashion of God taking the initiative in saving His people from their sins. There is the well-known invitation in Isaiah 1:18, which we have used as an alternate text for Septuagesima Sunday. There is the equally glorious declaration in Isaiah 43:25 (see verses 25-27), "I, I am He who blots out your transgressions for my own sake, and I will not remember your sins." This would make an excellent text for the Third Sunday after Trinity. It speaks a message that scarcely needs explanation. The Eisenach Old Testament selection is Isaiah 12, a song of thanksgiving for God's salvation, and this too would make an acceptable text; but we have assigned it to the fourth day of prayer (Thanksgiving). A very good text would be Isaiah 55:6-9, our Sexagesima text.

Our choice, however, is Isaiah 44:21-23, especially verse 22: "I have swept away your transgressions like a cloud; and your sins like mist; return to me, for I have redeemed you." These words are an illustration of God's prevenient and forgiving grace in terms of Israel in the Babylonian Captivity. We can learn from it "by way of example"; for God is ever the same, " a God merciful and gracious, slow to anger, and abounding in stedfast love and faithfulness, keeping stedfast love for thousands, forgiving iniquity and transgression and sin" (Exodus 34:6, 7). The redemption of Israel had, of course, a temporal aspect; but it had a spiritual aspect too: as the covenant people of God they had been sent into captivity because they had sinned and proved themselves to be a faithless servant; their redemption must therefore involve a return to the Lord, and the invitation or the admonition to return is based on God's readiness to forgive.

The text does not teach forgiveness apart from, or prior to repentance. It does offer the certainty of forgiveness as an inducement to repent, or to return. The approach is the same as when Paul says in Romans 2:4 that "God's kindness is meant to lead you to repentance." What good would repentance do without the assurance of a forgiving God? It was to His goodness that God appealed in trying to persuade Israel to return unto Him. It is to His love for us in Christ Jesus our Lord that we turn for the strongest appeal for repentance as well as faith today. It is because God is what He is, and does what He does, "forgiving iniquity and transgression and sin," that men are moved still to seek Him, and to know that their seeking is not vain. It is because God forgives that we can have the joy of salvation.

Basic religious teachings of the text:

1. The concept of God as a forgiving God, and of the gracious forgiveness of sins as an experience of His people.

2. God's call to Israel, and to the Church, to be His servant.

3. God's promise that He will not forget nor forsake His people if with all their heart they truly seek Him (see Jeremiah 29:12, 13).

4. God's invitation to His sinful people to return to Him and be forgiven, and to live in renewed covenant fellowship with Him, that He may be glorified in them as His redeemed people.

5. The song of joy that accompanies salvation, whether from earthly affliction or from the bondage of sin.

New Testament echoes of the text:

1. The language of Acts 3:19, "Repent therefore, and turn again, that your sins may be blotted out," is reminiscent of Isaiah 44:22. The similarity is more evident in ASV than in RSV.

2. The concept of redemption in Isaiah is not limited to the redemption from Babylon, not even to the spiritual aspects of that redemption, but points beyond to a perfect redemption experience that shall usher in the time of consummation of God's kingdom and of His covenant purpose. Because of its own inadequacy to accomplish the result which the prophecy seems to visualize the partial fulfilment in the return from Babylon is also seen to point beyond itself to a greater redemption experience in the future. It is in the light of redemptive history that the prophecy thus links up with the redemption concept in the New Testament. See I Peter 1:18, 19.

Fourth Sunday After Trinity

Topic for the Day: "The Judgments of Men and of God."

Text: Isaiah 3:13-15.

Theme: The Lord will enter into judgment.

Relation of the text to the topic:

The teaching of Jesus concerning the mote and the beam (Luke 6: 36-42) is the keynote to the lessons for the Fourth Sunday after Trinity. In terms of "our Christian life" (the general theme for the Trinity season of the Church year) we are warned against an unkind, or an untrue, or an unjust judgment of our neighbor, and are reminded of the just judgment of God, before whom each one of us shall give account of himself.

The New Testament lessons have reference especially to that sort of judgment which is expressed in words, and which reflects an opinion and an attitude; but, as seen from the story of the woman taken in adultery, wrong attitudes quickly and easily lead over into wrong actions against the one who has been judged to be a sinner. Hence, our Isaiah text, though different in emphasis, does not take us far afield. It has reference to the judgments of the rulers and elders in Israel, which perverted justice, and led to the confiscation of the property of the defenceless poor, and to general oppression of God's people. Whether it be unjust judgment in word and attitude, or in oppressive actions under the pretence of law and justice. God's word warns His people to have no part of it. God will judge them who presume to sit in judgment over others. He will judge those who judge unrighteously, and who oppress others under the pretext of a legal right.

There is nothing in any of the lessons for the day that would rule out the proper administration of law in the community, or that would hinder the bringing of the transgressor against that community to the bar of justice. There is warning against injustice, and against a fault-finding spirit, that is critical of the actions of others while slow to see anything wrong with oneself. If sin must be pointed out, it should be done in love, and for purposes of correction. If transgression must be punished, judgment should as far as possible be tempered with mercy, in the hope of redeeming the transgressor from his ways. If two are in disagreement, and appeal is made to the law of the land to decide between them, let justice prevail. For if we judge hastily, or if injustice is done by our human judgments, we need to be reminded that the final judgment is God's, and that each of us is accountable to Him alone; we are accountable to Him for every false or unjust judgment of our fellowman, in thought, word, or deed: we are accountable for every word that is not spoken in love as well as in truth.

Another appropriate text for this Sunday is Isaiah 42:18-25. The Eisenach Old Testament selection, Isaiah 65:17-19, 24-25, seems less appropriate.

Basic religious teachings of the text:

1. The unjust judgments of men, leading so often to injustice and oppression.

The entering of God into judgment with them who are guilty of unjust judgment of their fellowmen, whether in attitude or in action, in word or in deed.

3. The concern of God for the poor and the oppressed, who are the victims of man's unkindness and injustice in any form.

New Testament echoes of the text:

James 2:6 reveals the same concern as our text for the poor, who are dishonored and oppressed, and dragged wrongfully before the judgment-seats, of legal courts or of public opinion.

Fifth Sunday After Trinity

TOPIC FOR THE DAY: "Discipleship."

TEXT: Isaiah 54:11-17.

THEME: All your sons shall be taught by the Lord.

Relation of the text to the topic:

A disciple is a pupil or scholar, or one who is taught by a teacher (Matthew 10:24). He is also a follower of his teacher, being obedient to the teaching. In the American Standard Version of the book of Isaiah we find the word *disciples* three times: once in the text (8:16), and twice in the margin (50:4 and 54:13). In each instance it is the translation of the Hebrew passive verb meaning "them that are taught." Jesus made reference to Isaiah 54:13, when He said, "It is written in the prophets, "and they shall all be taught by God" (John 6:45). He added interpretatively, "Every one who has heard and learned from the Father comes to me." That is, they who are taught of God become the disciples of Jesus Christ.

We can readily see that Isaiah 54:13 makes a good text for a sermon on the theme of discipleship. We should not lose sight of its prophetic character. Together with the whole chapter of which it is a part it predicts a day when the spiritual aims and purposes of God's covenant with Israel shall have been fully attained. It visualizes a day like the one spoken of in Isaiah 11:9, when "the earth shall be full of the knowledge of the Lord as the waters cover the sea." The context indicates that the result of this universal knowledge of God will be universal peace. The secret of true inward peace is a real experiential knowledge of God; and the prophecy foresees the day when "all your sons" shall be taught of God, and shall share in the spiritual blessings of knowing Him as their Lord.

This experience was not unknown to God's people under the old covenant; but the words of the prophet here resemble those of Jeremiah in chapter 31:31-34, the prediction of "a new covenant," when "they shall all know me, from the least of them to the greatest, says the Lord." The relation between the old and the new covenant is not that of a sharp antithesis but of a fulfilment, so that the new covenant far transcends and surpasses the old. To this fulfilment the prophets are constantly looking forward, and the present experience is a promise of greater things to come. Without minimizing the significance of verse 13 in the past experience of Israel, the true application of the verse is to them who through the teaching of God are persuaded to come unto Christ, and to become his disciples, and to know his peace; for this belongs to the ultimate fulfilment of the covenant with Abraham. The essentials of Christian discipleship can be seen in this prophetic word.

Basic religious teachings of the text:

1. The nature of true discipleship: to be taught of God (vs. 13). Taught not only to know the truth, but to believe and to do it.

2. The result of a true knowledge of God, or of being taught of God: an experience of peace (vs. 13b: Hebrew shalom, RSV prosperity; ASV peace). The reference is to inward peace, first of all; but also to the blessing of external peace and prosperity to a God-fearing people. Comfort for those who are "storm-tossed" is found only in a living knowledge of God and a firm faith in His promises. That is true whatever the nature of the storm. Verse 11 may refer to both inward and outward affliction, as of the captivity. The promise is directed to the total life-situation.

3. The heritage of God's people under the covenant of blessing and peace (vs. 17). This truth applies to Israel and to the Church alike, insofar as they let themselves be taught of God so as to be truly His disciples.

New Testament echoes of the text:

1. The description of the foundations and the pinnacles and the gates in verses 11 and 12 in terms of fair colors and precious stones resembles the description of the foundations and the gates of the new Jerusalem in Revelation 21:19-21.

2. The reference to verse 13 in John 6:45, already noted.

3. The concept of security for God's people (vs. 17a) and of a heritage (vs. 17b) harmonizes with the New Testament concept of the sure victory of the kingdom of God.

Sixth Sunday After Trinity

Topic for the Day: "The Law of God."

Text: Isaiah 5:8-23.

Theme: He looked for righteousness.

Relation of the text to the topic:

The law of God has a definite place in our Christian life, not only to convict us of sin, but also to guide us in the way of righteousness. "The law is holy, and the commandment is holy and just and good," says Paul in Romans 7:12. Though I am free from its condemnation through faith in Christ, I am not free to ignore its directives; for that would be to disobey the will of God. Jesus did not destroy the law, nor did he abrogate its demands for righteousness, nor did he contradict the teaching of Moses in Deuteronomy 10:12, 13, that God gave His commandments for our good. John says of God's commandments that they "are not burdensome" (I John 5:3). When we love God, and live in true covenant fellowship with Him by faith in Jesus Christ as our Saviour, we discover that even His requirements are good.

It is against this background that we must consider and present the theme of God's law in relation to the Christian life. It always functions in a twofold way, convicting us of unrighteousness and sin, and leading us in the way of God's will and of righteousness of life. We can obey it in part, so that it truly is for our good, and for the good of our neighbor, here on earth; we cannot obey it so perfectly that we thereby inherit eternal life. But God is concerned that His people practise righteousness and shun unrighteousness in every human relationship. God speaks to the Christian conscience through His Moral Law and guides him in his daily conduct. For that reason the Augustana lectionary rightly includes a portion of Isaiah 5 as a lesson for this Sixth Sunday after Trinity, whose theme is the law of God.

The introductory paragraph in the chapter is the parable of the vineyard, which ends with this interpretative statement, "For the vineyard of the Lord of hosts is the house of Israel, and the men of Judah are his pleasant planting; and he looked for justice, but behold, bloodshed; for righteousness, but behold, a cry" (vs. 7). God looked for righteousness, but did not find it. Instead He found in Israel the flagrant examples of unrighteousness denounced by the six Woes that follow the parable, and that constitute our text. Covetousness and insatiable greed, drunken revels and dissipation, blasphemous unbelief, moral confusion, self-conceit, and the ambition to excel in drinking wine and in doing wickedness, are put under the Woe of God by the prophet. They need to be put there by the modern preacher as well. But at the same time our preaching should set forth the life of righteousness which God seeks in His people, and which is the spiritual fruit of a right relationship with Him. We need to be taught what is right as well as what is wrong, and to see our calling as Christians in the full light of God's law of love. For love is the fulfilment of the law: love finds the right answers to the perplexing ethical problems of the modern life-situations.

Basic religious teachings of the text:

1. The Woe of God on the sin of landgrabbing; the accumulation of wealth at the expense of our neighbor (vs. 8-10). The sin of "insatiable greed."

2. The Woe of God on drunken revelries and dissipation; rampant self-indulgence (vs. 11-17).

3. The Woe of God on the sin of blasphemous unbelief (vs. 18-19). "Bitter sarcasm — a bold figure," says Delitzsch. "Daring defiance against Jehovah," says George L. Robinson. The agelong blasphemy: "Let God prove His power *to me!"*

4. The Woe of God on moral crookedness (vs. 20). "The confusion of moral distinctions" (George L. Robinson). Sin itself defended, because conscience has been warped: the extremity of sin.

5. The Woe of God on the sin of self-conceit (vs. 21).

6. The Woe of God on them who are mighty in drinking wine and in doing wickedness (vs. 22-23).

New Testament echoes of the text:

1. The sin of covetousness is denounced in Ephesians 5:3-5.

2. The language of Jesus in Matthew 23:38, "your house is forsaken and desolate," seems to show familiarity with Isaiah 5:9, "many houses shall be desolate."

3. The attitude of mockery in II Peter 3:3, 4, is the same as in Isaiah 5:18, 19.

4. The teaching of Jesus in Matthew 6:22, 23, and in Luke 11:34, 35, resembles Isaiah 5:20 in that it refers to the confusion of moral distinctions.

5. Paul's admonition in Romans 12:16, "never be conceited," reflects the same attitude as the Woe in Isaiah 5:21. The difference is in the approach: Paul seeks to guide in the right way, whereas Isaiah denounces those who walk in the wrong way.

6. There is a marked parallelism between the words of James 5:6 and the words of Isaiah 5:23.

Seventh Sunday After Trinity

TOPIC FOR THE DAY: "God's Never-failing Providence."

TEXT: Isaiah 62:6-9.

THEME: Believing prayer reminds the Lord of His promises.

Relation of the text to the topic:

In the outline of the church year given by Bo Giertz in his book for confirmands, "Grunden," the day of the Transfiguration of Christ takes the place of the Seventh Sunday after Trinity. That is also true in the Augustana lectionary. If the Seventh Sunday after Trinity be observed, the theme of "God's never-failing providence" seems to be an appropriate one. The theme is suggested by the Collect for the day: "O God, whose never-failing providence ordereth all things both in heaven and earth: We humbly beseech Thee to put away from us all hurtful things, and to give us those things which be profitable for us."

God's providence to which appeal is here made implies Divine provision for all our needs. It points to God as the source of every good and perfect gift. That includes provision for our temporal and bodily needs. The Old Gospel text for the day is the story of the feeding of the 4000. Another text in the ELC lectionary is the twenty-third psalm. Other lessons stress the spiritual gifts, such as eternal life, and the forgiveness of sins, and righteousness by faith. The gracious provision of

God for all our needs, both temporal and spiritual, is the over-all message and theme of God's word for this day.

In harmony with this theme Isaiah 41:17-20 would make a good text; see the Fourth Sunday in Lent. The text that we have selected is Isaiah 62;6-9, and the chief reason for the choice is God's promise to Israel in verses 8 and 9. Like so many other prophecies, it seems to have an eschatological significance, and to refer to "the latter days," even to "the times of restoration of all things" (Acts 3:21). It may be that there is reference also to a nearer intermediate experience, and that the shortened perspective of prophecy comes into play, combining near and distant events into one picture. Be that as it may, the promise is that in that future day God's people shall no more suffer lack of anything, but shall eat and drink, and shall praise the Lord in peaceful enjoyment of the good gifts of His providence. The watchmen upon the walls are called "Jehovah's remembrancers" (ASV), who remind God in prayer of these promises that He has given; and they are urged to take no rest, and to give God no rest, until He establish His promises by fulfilling them.

But though the prophecy is forward-looking, we do see in it a principle which has spiritual relevancy also in the present. God will provide for the needs of His people, and they have reason to praise Him even now for His never-failing providence. God wants us to be His remembrancers, so that we remind Him of His promises and base our prayers upon them. He wants us to have the confidence in Him of which Jesus spoke in the Sermon on the Mount. The Lord will provide. If He should withhold some of His blessings for a season, we may be sure there is a good reason for so doing; and we cling to the assurance that it is His gracious and good will to bless His people with peace and prosperity. We recognize it as a token of His favor when we as a people are permitted to harvest what we have planted, and to eat what we have harvested, and to give God praise for the abundance with which He supplies our daily bread.

Basic religious teachings of the text:

1. God wants to be reminded of His promises by the prayers of His people, even in temporal things.

2. There are those who as watchmen upon the walls of Zion are called to be in a special way "Jehovah's remembrancers" in a ministry of intercessory prayer.

3. What God has promised, that He will also perform, and He will establish His word.

4. God's purpose with the faithful keeping of His promises is to make His people who trust in those promises a praise in the earth, and to receive praise from His people.

5. God's providence is a present as well as a future reality.

New Testament echoes of the text:

There is no direct reference to it in the New Testament, but its teaching of God's faithfulness to His promises and of Divine provision for His people is New Testament teaching also.

The Transfiguration of Christ

TOPIC FOR THE DAY: "On the Mount of Transfiguration."

TEXT: Isaiah 49:7.

THEME: The servant who was despised is exalted and glorified.

Relation of the text to the topic:

There is no prophecy in the Old Testament that speaks specifically of the Transfiguration as an event and experience in the life of the Messiah. The closest that we can come to it is by way of the concept of his glory. We recall the words in John 12:41, "Isaiah said this because he saw his glory and spoke of him." We recall also what Peter says about the experience with Jesus in the holy mount: "For when he received honor and glory from God the Father and the voice was borne to him by the Majestic Glory, 'This is my beloved Son, with whom I am well pleased,' we heard this voice borne from heaven, for we were with him on the holy mountain." (II Peter 1:17, 18). A prophecy that reveals the glory of the Messiah would therefore make an appropriate text for the day of Christ's Transfiguration, and so would a prophecy that indicates God's acknowledgment of him as His servant; and even a prophecy that speaks of a future revelation of the glory of God, for in the light of the fulfilment this is also the glory of Christ (see II Corinthians 4:6).

The text that we have selected is of the second kind, a testimony by God concerning His servant which reveals both his humiliation and his exaltation. It does not contain the word *glory,* but it is nevertheless a prediction of honor and glory. It is spoken to the servant in his state of humiliation; it assures him that even the great of the earth shall one day come to worship him. The humiliation-exaltation motif is evident, and the exaltation theme fits Transfiguration Day as well as Ascension Day. But we must be careful in our preaching lest we make the prophecy more specific in its reference than it is. It is the major outlines rather than the detailed incidents of Messiah's life that are set forth in prophecy. It was primarily of "the sufferings of Christ and subsequent glory" (I Peter 1:11) that the Spirit of Christ which was in the prophets testified; and their testimony was in "many fragments" (Weymouth's translation of Hebrews 1:1), in contrast to that of the Son, who "brightly reflects God's glory" (Weymouth, Hebrews 1:3). That is why many an Old Testament text takes on new luster and clarity when seen in the light of the completed life-portrait of Christ in the Gospels. That is why Isaiah 49:7 *as a prophecy* clarified in its meaning *by history* makes a good text if we wish to preach of Christ's glory as the Father glorified him in his life as a servant by voicing His approval, and as he is now glorified when men worship him.

Basic religious teachings of the text:

1. "Thus says the Lord": this is the word of the Lord.
2. "The servant of rulers": the servant in his humiliation.
3. "They shall worship" (ASV): the servant in his exaltation.
4. "Because of the Lord, who is faithful": this is the work of the Lord, who is faithful to His covenant.
5. "Who has chosen you": the Divine approbation of the Messiah.

New Testament echoes of the text:

The humiliation and the exaltation of the servant as seen in the life of Jesus Christ, who is called both the Son and the Servant of God.

Eighth Sunday After Trinity

Topic for the Day: "Error" (or, Beware of False Prophets.)
Text: Isaiah 28:14-22.
Theme: Be not scoffers!

Relation of the text to the topic:

The message for the Christian life in most of the lessons for this day is a warning to beware of false prophets and to prove the spirits, "whether they are of God." (I John 4:1). The purpose is that we may know how to discern the difference between "the spirit of truth, and the spirit of error," and that we may choose the right way, which is the way of faith in Jesus Christ and of obedience to the will of God.

Our text from Isaiah is right in line with this theme and purpose; for it speaks of scoffers who make lies their refuge, and directs to these scoffers a stern warning of destruction if they persist in their scornful attitude towards God's word of truth. The historical situation is that of the reign of Hezekiah, when on the political and military horizon there was the constant threat from Assyria. There was an influential party in Judah that wished to bring in Egypt as an ally in resisting the Assyrian aggression (see chapters 30 and 31). The prophet's message from God was that they should put less confidence in "entangling alliances" and have more faith in God. If they were more concerned about the spiritual and moral health of the nation, they would not need to worry so much about political or military foes from without. There was a reason to be concerned about the spiritual and moral health of the nation in view of the situation described in verses 7 and 8; a situation which seems to have prevailed in both the northern and the southern kingdoms. At any rate, many of the rulers in Jerusalem mockingly rejected the prophet's preaching (vs. 9, 10) and continued to put their confidence in men instead of in God. The prophet characterizes their action by representing them as saying, "We have made a covenant with death" (vs. 15). That is about what the alliance with Egypt amounted to. By way of contrast he presents in verse 16 the sure foundation on which they ought to build their hopes. The sure foundation, and the precious cornerstone, refer first of all to the covenant assurance of the presence of God with His people and the primary need therefore of faith in God; but, as with so many aspects of the covenant, this truth of the presence of God found a larger fulfilment in Christ, and we can see a Messianic aspect to this prophetic word even though its fundamental message to Israel was the need of faith in God. If they refused to put their faith in God, and insisted on trusting in Egypt instead, they would learn by bitter experience that "the bed is too short to stretch oneself on it, and the covering too narrow to wrap oneself in it" (vs. 20).

The spirit of error as seen in this setting has a distinctly modern flavor; for we too are prone to put our confidence in man rather than in God, and to be more concerned about political threats to our safety than we are about the spiritual and moral threats. The spirit of truth points here, as also in the New Testament texts for the day, to faith in God, and to the life obedient to His will. Another text that could be used to bring out the contrast between the spirit of error and the spirit of truth is Isaiah 30:8-16.

Basic religious teachings of the text:

1. The only sure foundation is the one that God has laid, first in His covenant of blessing with Abraham, and then, in fulfilment of that covenant, in Christ. "He who believes will not be in haste"; the haste of those who turn frantically to seek refuge and help everywhere but where it can be found.

2. The confidence in human devices, human alliances, and human strength, which leaves God out, is like a covenant with death, for it leads to destruction for nations as well as for individuals.

3. The admonition, "do not scoff" (vs. 22: ASV, "be not scoffers"), is always relevant.

4. The failure of human plans brings discomfort and distress (vs. 20).

New Testament echoes of the text:

1. In Romans 9:33, Isaiah 8:14 and 28:16 seem to be combined in one quotation. The ultimate spiritual fulfilment of both is seen to be in Christ. That is not evident on the face of the prophecy; but the covenant with Abraham, and with Israel, included Christ, even as the oak is in the acorn. God's covenant promise is the foundation, and faith builds on that promise.

2. Is Romans 10:11 also a reference to Isaiah 28:16 (see ASV margin)? See also I Peter 2:6. This is not a case of literal quotation of

a prediction but rather of spiritual interpretation and application. Prophecy is fulfilled, but along the lines indicated previously.

3. Ephesians 2:20, the chief cornerstone, and I Corinthians 3:11, the foundation, may reflect Isaiah 28:16 as well as Psalm 118:22. See also Matthew 21:42; Mark 12:10; Luke 20:17; Acts 4:11. In the last-mentioned four passages the reference is to Psalm 118:22.

Ninth Sunday After Trinity

TOPIC FOR THE DAY: "The Responsibility of Stewardship."

TEXT: Isaiah 9:13-17.

THEME: Those who lead this people lead them astray.

Relation of the text to the topic:

The theme of Stewardship has many angles. It is not limited to the stewardship of money, but may include the stewardship of time, of talents, and even of life itself. It may be considered from the viewpoint of the responsibility of the Christian minister and teacher, who is a steward of "the mysteries of God" (I Corinthians 4:1) and of "God's varied grace" (I Peter 4:10), or a steward of spiritual things, which he is to minister unto the people of God. Of such stewardship Paul says, "It is required of stewards that they be found trustworthy" (I Corinthians 4:2). Of such stewardship the Lord speaks in Luke 12:42, "Who then is the faithful and wise steward, whom his master will set over his household, to give them their portion of food at the proper time?" Even the parable of the unrighteous steward (Luke 16:1-9), which is the Old Gospel text for the day, may involve something of this aspect of stewardship. It is brought out most vividly, however, in the lesson from Luke 12:42-48, both in the opening question quoted above, and in the description that follows of the faithful and of the unfaithful servant or steward. The faithful steward gives to his master's household "their portion of food at the proper time." The unfaithful steward is represented as saying in his heart, "My master is delayed in coming," and as mistreating instead of providing for his fellow-servants.

It is this same picture of unfaithful stewardship that we find in Isaiah 9:13-17 in terms of the spiritual leaders of Israel. These leaders feed the people with lies, and lead them astray. There is a close connection between last Sunday's theme of *error* and this Sunday's theme of *stewardship*, for unfaithful stewardship leads to error. We could have selected as our text a portion of the same chapter from which the text on error was taken; for there is in Isaiah 28:7-8 a description of spiritual leaders, both priests and prophets, who are overcome with strong drink, and who consequently err in vision and stumble in judgment. Another appropriate text might be Isaiah 42:18-24, where the Lord's servant is pictured as blind, and His messenger as deaf, and the result is general disobedience to the Lord's teaching; for as Hosea says, "like people, like priest" (Hosea 4:9).

The truth learned from this Old Testament situation can readily be applied in preaching to the situation today: it is required of everyone to whom has been given the stewardship of spiritual things such as God's Word that he be faithful; faithful to the Lord, faithful to the word of truth, and faithful in providing for the needs of each member of the spiritual household of God. If the steward fails in his responsibility, the whole household suffers.

Basic religious teachings of the text:

1. If spiritual leaders teach lies, the people are caused to err; and it leads to general wickedness and evil-doing, and in the end to destruction.

2. The anger of the Lord is directed against every false and faithless steward, as it was against the elder and the prophet in Israel who spoke lies, and He will cut them off from His people.

3. If men who presume to speak for God speak lies, the people will not be apt to turn unto God and seek Him (vs. 13). The responsibility of stewardship is great because it involves others besides ourselves.

New Testament echoes of the text:

1. The phrase "in one day" is sufficiently unusual (see also Isaiah 47:9) to make its use in Revelation 18:8 in reference to the fall of Babylon seem like a conscious borrowing of the prophet's language to fit a new situation.

2. The picture of false prophets who teach lies is common in the Old Testament, and Jesus warns against such false prophets and false Christs in the New Testament (Matthew 24:24).

3. The saying of Jesus in Matthew 15:14 concerning blind guides fits both the text from Isaiah 9 and the one in Isaiah 42:18 ff. See also Matthew 23:16, 24, and context.

Tenth Sunday After Trinity

TOPIC FOR THE DAY: "Wasted Opportunities."

TEXT: Isaiah 65:1-7.

THEME: A rebellious people.

Relation of the text to the topic:

There is a marked resemblance between this text and the Old Gospel text, the story of Jesus weeping over Jerusalem. In fact, Jesus might well have used the very words of Isaiah 65:2 to describe the situation which caused him such grief: "I spread out my hands all the day to a rebellious people, who walk in a way that is not good, following their own devices." Both texts describe wasted spiritual opportunities. So does also the lesson from Matthew 11:20-24, where Jesus upbraids the unrepentant cities of Chorazin, Bethsaida, and Capernaum. The rejection of Jesus at Nazareth, Luke 4:23-30, illustrates the same truth; and so does the evil, unbelieving heart against which we are warned in Hebrews 3:12. The whole history of Israel as recorded in the Bible is largely one of wasted or of rejected opportunities. Is it not often true of the Christian Church also, that the Lord pleads in vain for that "closer walk with God," while we walk "in a way that is not good," indifferent to His invitation to live our lives in intimate daily fellowship with Him?

The particular thing that is involved in our wrong attitudes may vary according to circumstances; but the basic factors of unbelief and of disobedience, and of choosing our own way in preference to God's way, remain constant. The Isaiah text indicates idolatry and the abominations of heathen worship as the way in which God's covenant people chose to walk. The Old Gospel text, which includes a reference to the cleansing of the temple, indicates that there was a definite lack of concern for spiritual things, such as prayer. Both texts predict judgment as the inevitable result.

It is interesting to note that the words in verse 5, which ASV renders "for I am holier than thou" and RSV "for I am set apart from you," represent the attitude of these apostates from the religion of the LORD (Jehovah) who had become initiated into "heathen mysteries" and looked down upon the simple folks who still worshipped Jehovah. To us a holier-than-thou attitude suggests the Pharisee rather than the apostate; yet, they have this in common that they both lay claim to superior holiness or to a higher level of religious attainment. In both instances there is revealed a lack of knowledge of the true God. Both are guilty of walking "in a way that is not good" and of following "their own devices." The humble faith of the contrite sinner in God's forgiving mercy, and sincere obedience to God's righteous will for our lives, are the marks of those who have not wasted their spiritual opportunities.

Basic religious teachings of the text:

1. The faithful love of God in pleading "all the day" with His rebellious people to walk in His ways for their own good.

2. The poignant description, from God's point of view, of His people's rebellious attitude and foolish apostasy, which only leads to ruin.

3. If we do not walk with God, we walk in a way that is not good. See Jeremiah 6:16.

4. If men persist in iniquity, they will learn that the Lord repays their iniquities "into their bosom."

5. The tragedy of wasted spiritual opportunities.

New Testament echoes of the text:

1. In Romans 10:20, 21, Paul applies the first verse of Isaiah 65 to the Gentiles and the second verse to Israel. The latter interpretation is self-evident. There is, however, some difficulty both of translation and of interpretation in verse one. There is nothing in the context to indicate a direct reference to the Gentiles. Dummelow says that Paul "applies the passage by inference to the heathen world." This would be in line with his treatment of other passages such as the two Hosea quotations in Romans 9. To recognize in a prophecy a principle which permits of application to a new and perhaps a wider situation is not a denial of the truth of the prophecy. But in the case of Isaiah 65:1 it must be admitted that the most natural translation of the text is that in AV, and that when so translated it fits the situation among the Gentiles better than the one among the Jews. One could wish in this instance that RSV had simply translated the text instead of trying to interpret it, even though the interpretation that it adopts is followed by many modern versions (see the Swedish, Moffatt's, AJV). Even as translated by RSV it fits the situation of Gentile as well as Jewish rebellion. It is

one of the marvels of God's patient grace that He keeps on saying, "Here am I, here am I," to them that do not seek Him; and the equally marvelous truth is that because of His seeking them He is often found by them who did not seek Him.

2. The "holier-than-thou" attitude of verse 5 (see ASV) has its counterpart in the New Testament: see Matthew 9:11: Luke 7:39; Luke 18:9-12.

Eleventh Sunday After Trinity

TOPIC FOR THE DAY: "True and False Righteousness."

TEXT: Isaiah 1:10-17.

THEME: A wrong and a right kind of religious life.

Relation of the text to the topic:

The antithesis between true and false righteousness in the evengelical sense is the antithesis between the publican and the Pharisee in Jesus' parable. True righteousness is where faith in God and in His forgiving mercy is reckoned to the sinner for righteousness. False righteousness is really self-righteousness, where a man trusts in himself, and especially in his own religious acts, as if they made him righteous. The key to the difference is the humble and contrite heart.

The antithesis presented by the prophet is a slightly different but a closely related one. This is one of several passages in the Old Testament where we find an alleged conflict between priest and prophet, or between priestly religion and prophetic religion. The former is said to be characterized by formalistic ritualism; the latter by ethical righteousness. Actually the conflict is not between priestly and prophetic religion per se, but between a ritual religion that has sunk to the level of pure formalism and has completely neglected or ignored the claims of the Moral Law, and the prophetic preaching of ethical righteousness as a fruit of a right relationship with God. God cannot stand the combination of "wickedness and worship" in the religious life. The ritual worship of Israel, which seemingly was offered in abundance, did not please God because it was divorced from real concern for those weightier matters of the law stressed by Jesus in Matthew 23:23, "justice and mercy and faith."

Our religion may not be made a cloak for unrighteousness of life. The righteousness ascribed to the publican on the strength of his prayer, "God, be merciful to me a sinner," did not justify him in continuing in sin. True righteousness includes the fruit of good works. The prophecy of Isaiah does not teach work-righteousness, but it is a powerful demand for ethical righteousness in our religion. We have no right to empty the Biblical concept of righteousness in the Christian life, so as to make justification by faith a substitute for sanctification of life. "You will know them by their fruits," said Jesus; and down through the years, the Biblical and Christian emphasis on righteousness has been one of the strongest evidences of the truth of the religion that we profess. There is no antithesis between a true spiritual and a right ethical emphasis in religion, or between faith and life in Christianity. It is only a matter of giving to each its proper place. True righteousness begins with a humble faith in God as our Saviour, and is a gift from Him; true righteousness expresses itself in a life that is obedient to the will of God in every ethical relationship, and is therefore an experience of God's power to sanctify and to redeem our lives from the power of evil.

Another good text for this Sunday is Isaiah 66:1-4; see the antithesis between him "that is humble and contrite in spirit, and trembles at my word," and the formalist in religion who brought his sacrifices in the wrong spirit and delighted in them though God calls them "abominations." Of the former God says, "this is the man to whom I will look"; of the latter He says, "when I called, no one answered, when I spoke they did not listen; but they did what was evil in my eyes, and chose that in which I did not delight." Formalism in religion and ritual ceremonies are insufficient for righteousness. True righteousness is both spiritual and ethical in its nature, and requires a living faith and sincere obedience.

Basic religious teachings of the text:

1. The Divine authority in prophetic preaching: the word of the Lord, the law or teaching of our God. The prophets were spokesmen for God.

2. The emphatic Divine rejection of a sacrificial worship that is not performed in the right spirit; which is content with formalism, without concern for the spiritual and the moral life. As Delitzsch says, "Because they had not performed what Jehovah commanded as He commanded it, He expressly forbids them to continue it."

3. The emphatic declaration of Divine attitude: "I cannot endure iniquity and solemn assembly" (G. A. Smith, "wickedness and worship").

4. The emphatic Divine demand for ethical righteousness as a part of true religion, with justice and mercy as major examples of such righteousness.

New Testament echoes of the text:

1. In Revelation 11:8 as in Isaiah 1:10 Jerusalem is referred to as Sodom, because its spiritual character was like that of Sodom.

2. The admonition in Romans 12:9, "hate what is evil, hold fast to what is good," shows marked similarity to that of Isaiah, "cease to do evil, learn to do good." See also Amos 5:14, 15.

3. The concern for the fatherless and the widow that is enjoined in Isaiah 1:17 is seen also in the definition of pure religion in James 1:27.

Twelfth Sunday After Trinity

TOPIC FOR THE DAY: "The Use of the Tongue."

TEXT: Isaiah 29:13-16.

THEME: Worshipping God with the lips and not with the heart.

Relation of the text to the topic:

The emphasis on a right use of the tongue is quite evident in most of the lessons for this Sunday. The Old Gospel text is the story of the healing of the deaf-mute. The Gospel from Matthew 12:33-37 stresses the accountability of men for every idle word that they shall speak. The theme of one of the Epistles, James 3:8-12, is the taming of the tongue.

Either Isaiah 29:13-16 or Isaiah 29:18-21, the Eisenach Old Testament selection, harmonizes with this general theme for the day. Perhaps the two could be joined together in one longer text. In verse 13 the Lord rebukes the hypocrisy of religion and worship which consists only of words. The marginal translation in ASV, which both AJV and RSV adopt, interprets the meaning of the last line of the verse correctly, "their fear of me is a commandment of men learned by rote." They know the words, but they do not know God. They honor God with their lips but not with their heart. That is a wrong use of the tongue. It would not help matters, of course, to keep silent with their lips; for their real trouble was with their heart, and that would be just as far removed from God if they failed to worship altogether; but it is just as true that their words did not help matters either. The misuse of the tongue is not confined to swearing and cursing. It enters even into worship if there is no true knowledge of God, which shows itself in sincerity, and which leads to right action. Verse 15, on the other hand, represents the attitude of the scoffer (see also vs. 20), who does not even make a pretence of worshipping God. The scoffer dishonors God even with his words; for when he says, "Who sees us?", "Who knows us?", that is the same as to say, "Why bother with God? He doesn't count for anything!" The judgment of God on such an attitude is forcefully expressed in verse 16.

The Eisenach Old Testament text has more direct reference to the *right* use of words. Even though the scoffer may lay a snare for him and accuse him falsely, nevertheless the one "who reproves in the gate" is right in speaking the truth in love whenever there is need of such reproof. The meaning of the first line of verse 21 is not clear in the Hebrew text: AJV translates, "That make a man an offender by words"; but it is still not clear whether it refers to the words of false accusation, which make an innocent man seem to be an offender, or whether it refers to the words of the innocent one, which are twisted so as to make him seem to be the offender. RSV seems to follow the first line of interpretation: "who by a word make a man out to be an offender, and lay a snare for him who reproves in the gate, and with an empty plea turn aside him who is in the right." This would be a wrong use of the tongue in relation to our fellowmen. A right use of the tongue is suggested by verse 19; for the rejoicing of the poor and the meek in the Lord, the Holy One of Israel, is naturally expressed in words. Words of praise, sincerely spoken, are always God-pleasing. So are words spoken in truth and love in the human relationships.

Basic religious teachings of the text:

1. A God-pleasing worship must consist of more than words; the attitude of the heart comes first with God.

2. True religion is not something "learned by rote," where we parrot expressions that men have taught us, without knowing what they mean or letting them become a part of a vital religious experience.

3. We use words rightly when we worship God with prayer, praise, and thanksgiving.

4. God's verdict on the words of the scoffers is, "You turn things upside down!"

5. We should watch our words in relation to men as well as in relation to God and always have respect for the truth (vs. 21).

New Testament echoes of the text:

1. Jesus quotes verse 13, and applies the prophecy to his own situation; see Matthew 15:7-9 and Mark 7:6-7. There is a slight difference in wording; the essential meaning remains the same.

2. Paul shows familiarity with Isaiah 29:16 and applies it to a wider situation; see Romans 9:19-21.

3. Verse 18 may be one of several Old Testament prophecies that form the background for Jesus' words to John; see Matthew 11:4, 5, and Mark 7:37.

4. The Old Testament emphasis on the poor and the meek is echoed in the New Testament; see the Beatitudes (Matthew 5).

Thirteenth Sunday After Trinity

TOPIC FOR THE DAY: "Mercy."

TEXT: Isaiah 54:4-10.

THEME: With everlasting love I will have compassion on you.

Relation of the text to the topic:

Our text contains a glorious declaration of God's merciful intentions towards His people Israel. In the historical background we see the covenant blessing with Abraham, which became a covenant with Israel as the chosen people. Under the terms of that covenant the relationship between the Lord and His people is likened to that between husband and wife, a relationship of love. The second chapter of Hosea parallels this chapter closely in thought. Because of Israel's unfaithfulness to the covenant she became as "a wife forsaken" in the afflictions of the Babylonian Captivity. The prophecy contrasts this experience of affliction with the great mercy or compassion of God which they should experience, because God is faithful to His covenant. The affliction and the wrath, the condition where they seemed forsaken of God, was only "for a brief moment"; the promise for the future is, "with everlasting love I will have compassion (ASV mercy) on you."

The key-word is the Hebrew word *hesed,* which ASV usually renders as *lovingkindness* and AV as *mercy,* but which in RSV is usually translated as *steadfast love;* for *hesed* has not only the connotation of love and kindness but also of faithfulness to covenant. Closely associated with it in our text is the verb meaning "have mercy" (ASV) or "have compassion" (RSV). Love, mercy, compassion—what a trio of words to express the covenant character of God! For love and mercy are not a passing whim with God: they are a part of His covenant faithfulness; He is faithful to His covenant of blessing and of peace, and His is a steadfast love and a great compassion. The "hesed olam" (everlasting love) is reminiscent of the "berith olam" (an everlasting covenant) of Genesis 17. It seems to indicate that the prophecy is not limited to the historical situation where it takes its rise, but that it visualizes the whole covenant purpose and goal of God, and sums it up in the assurance that He has mercy or compassion on men. What is said of God in relation to Israel is true of God in relation to all men. God is merciful, and He desires mercy (see Hosea 6:6 and Matthew 9:13).

Though our Isaiah text speaks only of God's mercy, and the regular lessons for the day treat more of man's mercy, the connection between the two should be evident; for love is of God, who is love (I John 4:7, 8). It is the mercy of God towards us that moves us to be merciful towards others. It would be a mistake to preach on this or on any other text that speaks of God's mercy without emphasizing the practice of mercy in the Christian life. It would be a mistake also to preach on this or any other Old Testament text that reveals the character of God without applying it to ourselves. "God is like that," then, now, and always;

and this is His promise not only to Israel but to everyone who has become a child of the covenant, and a true son of Abraham, through faith in the Lord Jesus Christ. "The God of the whole earth he is called" (vs. 5).

Basic religious teachings of the text:

1. The Divine encouragement to His people: "Fear not, for you will not be ashamed" (vs. 4).

2. The covenant relationship: "For your Maker is your husband" (vs. 5); "for the Lord has called you like a wife forsaken and grieved in spirit, like a wife of youth when she is cast off" (vs. 6). A relationship of love; see Hosea 2 and Ephesians 5:22-33.

3. The possessive pronoun "your," indicating a personal relationship on the part of the believer: "your" Maker, "your" husband, "your" Redeemer, "your" God. In the background is the covenant promise to Abraham and his seed to be "their God" (Genesis 17:8).

4. The truth that present afflictions are not worthy to be compared with the great mercies which await us (see Romans 8:18 ff.).

5. The heart-warming promise in verse 8, which is "for us."

6. The covenant with Noah, faithfully fulfilled by God, a guarantee of the same faithful fulfilment of His covenant of peace.

7. The theology of the text, especially the statement "the Lord who has compassion on you."

New Testament echoes of the text:

Every word in it can be applied to Christ in relation to the Church, even though the primary reference is to the Lord (Jehovah) in relation to Israel.

Fourteenth Sunday After Trinity

TOPIC FOR THE DAY: "Gratitude."

TEXT: Isaiah 25:1-5.

THEME: I will praise my God, for He has done wonderful things.

Relation of the text to the topic:

The mercy of God not only moves the recipient to be merciful, it also moves him to be thankful. The mercy is expressed towards his fellowmen, the gratitude towards God. It is appropriate that one Sunday in the church year is devoted to the place of thankfulness and praise in the Christian life. The Old Gospel text, the story of the ten lepers that were cleansed, of whom only one returned to give thanks, should teach us that gratitude is not always commensurate with the gifts received, and should lead us to stress gratitude in our preaching as a genuine fruit of the Holy Spirit.

The ideal text from Isaiah would seem to be chapter 12, which is a song of thanksgiving: "I will give thanks to thee, O Lord" (vs. 1); "Give thanks to the Lord" (vs. 4). This song, however, we have reserved for Thanksgiving Day. The text selected is a song of praise for God's favor. Praise and thanksgiving are closely related, and neither is possible without the truly grateful heart. The gratitude and praise is for the wonderful things that God has done. Israel could think of these things in terms of her national history, from the Exodus onward. We can think of these things in terms of the whole Bible history, from the first Gospel promise, Genesis 3:15, to its glorious fulfilment as expressed in "the little Bible," John 3:16; and in terms of Church history too: for we see there throughout evidences of God's faithfulness and truth (vs. 1, ASV).

These last two words are two significant words in covenant theology. Both come from the Hebrew word *Amen,* and both stress this attribute of our God that He is faithful and trustworthy, and that His plans are "faithful and sure" (vs. 1, RSV). Surely that is occasion for gratitude on the part of His people! The illustrations that follow of the wonderful things that God has done are from the history of God's people in the Old Testament. Cities are reduced to ruins, and enemies are subdued, while a place of refuge and a stronghold are provided for the poor and needy. The language of verse 4 is at least partly metaphorical. It suggests a universal experience, and a universal promise, that God will be a stronghold and a refuge to His people in every time of need. It is out of such experience that true gratitude is born. We are thankful as we experience what God is, and what God has done, in relation to us. Being thankful, we will praise His name.

Basic religious teachings of the text:

1. The recognition of God as *my* God: personal faith.
2. The determination to exalt and to praise His name.

3. The reason for the praise in the wonderful things which God has done, and because His plans are faithful and sure.

4. The assurance that God is a place of refuge to the poor and needy, be they poor in spirit only, or be they such as suffer temporal need.

New Testament echoes of the text:

1. The reference to God's "plans formed of old" in relation to His covenant deeds (vs. 1) is similar to Paul's thought in Ephesians 1:11. See also Hebrews 6:17.

2. The concept of God as our refuge and strength is prominent in the Old Testament; it has its counterpart in many of the assuring promises of Jesus in the New Testament.

Fifteenth Sunday After Trinity

TOPIC FOR THE DAY: "Our Daily Bread."

TEXT: Isaiah 55:1-5.

THEME: Why do you spend your money for that which is not bread?

Relation of the text to the topic:

The theme "Our Daily Bread" may be somewhat misleading, since the primary emphasis in the lessons for the day is not on temporal things but on things that are spiritual and eternal. By way of illustration see Galatians 6:8; Matthew 6:33; Luke 10:41, 42; I Corinthians 7:29-31; and Matthew 6:19-20. With this emphasis our text is in perfect harmony; see especially verses 1 and 2. The teaching is similar to that of Deuteronomy 8:2-3, where the purpose of God's chastening as well as of His gracious provision during the forty years in the wilderness is said to have been this: "that he might make you know that man does not live by bread alone, but that man lives by everything that proceeds out of the mouth of the Lord." Notice the words, "by bread alone": for man does need bread also; he needs provision for his bodily life.

Through the lessons for this day runs the assurance that if we put first things first, God will take care of *all* our needs. Certainly that was true under the covenant with Israel, where material and spiritual blessings were so closely intertwined. There is a breadth about this prophecy in Isaiah 55 that corresponds to the breadth of God's covenant purpose from the beginning, which, rightly understood, includes the whole life of man. In preaching on this text we should emphasize the spiritual blessings promised, but we should not exclude the material and temporal. The same is true when we preach on Matthew 6:33. But in either case we should stress that "a man's life does not consist in the abundance of his possessions" (Luke 12:15). The concern for daily bread is simply *a part* of our human concern for those things which satisfy our human need. We need much more than food for our stomachs; we need also food for our souls. God has given priority to the latter as the more important of the two; but He has not forgotten that we need both. It is sufficient for Christian faith to know that God is gracious and will provide for all our needs. He is the giver of every good and perfect gift. He gives also our daily bread.

Basic religious teachings of the text:

1. That God's grace and goodness are always free. *God gives.* He does not sell His blessings, be they material or spiritual. The command to "buy" is qualified immediately by "without money and without price," for that is God's way.

2. That it is a mistake to put temporal things ahead of the spiritual, the affairs of this life ahead of the kingdom of God, our own interests ahead of God's will. There is no lasting satisfaction in life unless we hearken diligently unto God.

3. That man does not live by bread alone, but by every word that proceeds from the mouth of God. Faith and obedience are prerequisites to a life that is meaningful and satisfying.

4. That God has made an everlasting covenant with David, and that this covenant finds its ultimate fulfilment in Christ and in his gifts to men.

5. That through Christ the blessings of the covenant shall include all peoples.

6. That God glorifies His people by the gifts that He bestows upon them, and in the service that He enables them to perform for their God.

New Testament echoes of the text:

1. The invitation to the thirsty (vs. 1) resembles the invitation of Jesus in John 7:37; see also John 4:14.

2. Jesus' words in Matthew 10:8, "you received without pay, give without pay," is another way of stating the same truth as Isaiah does with the words "without money and without price."

3. The last line of verse 3 is quoted in Acts 13:34, with a slightly different wording, and applied to the resurrection of Jesus. The covenant with David was a Messianic covenant.

Sixteenth Sunday After Trinity

TOPIC FOR THE DAY: "The Shadow of Death."

TEXT: Isaiah 38 (especially vs. 18, 19).

THEME: I will praise the Lord as long as I live!

Relation of the text to the topic:

In terms of the Christian life, the lessons for this day aim to give comfort and hope to us who "are distressed by our enemy death." The story of Hezekiah's recovery from a sickness that seemed to be unto death is worthy of a place alongside the New Testament stories of the raising of Lazarus and of the widow of Nain's son, for it reveals the same power of God over life and death. It is true that the deliverance in Hezekiah's case came in the form of restored health after serious illness, while in the case of the others it came in the form of a resurrection from the dead. The words of the psalmist, "a prayer to the God of my life" (Psalm 42:8), are true in each situation; for He is "the God of my life" in more ways than one. He can help me to live courageously in faith. He can save me from death, if He will, even when death seems inevitable. He can raise me from the dead, and will do so at the last day. What joyous confidence should be ours who believe in the living God! What thankfulness that we may still praise God in the land of the living!

Hezekiah's words in verses 18, 19, should not be construed as a denial of a life after death, although admittedly the doctrine of the hereafter was made much clearer by the New Testament revelation. Hezekiah's intention is to stress that both the experience of God's truth (faithfulness) and the witness to that truth *here on earth* is ended by death. If God had permitted Hezekiah to die, it would have meant one less voice in the chorus of testimony and praise here on earth. For "the living, the living, he thanks thee, as I do this day; the father makes known to the children thy faithfulness." The life on earth has a vital place in the history of redemption; and the longing to live out our days is natural for us as Christians, if for no other reason than that we want to praise God here as long as our praise is needed. In Hezekiah's case this motive of praise played in with the normal human desire for life, and therefore he prayed unto the Lord, and the Lord heard his prayer and added fifteen years to his life.

The situation of Paul in Philippians 1:21-28 is not greatly different, although his concern to live is less for his own sake and more for the sake of others. Don't take Hezekiah as a perfect pattern in this matter of our attitude in sickness and in the hour of death, but recognize with him the power of God over life and death, and do not forget to pray and praise. We should receive thankfully each day and each year given us by Him who is the Lord over life and over death; we should pray even for health and length of days if it be God's will to grant it; but when we must go down into the valley of the shadow of death we should go in faith, fearing no evil, because the living God is with us and leads on through death into life. There is no shadow of death so dark but that it is illumined by Christian faith and hope in the promise of the ever-living, ever-present God, who says, "I have heard your prayer, I have seen your tears." We praise Him if He adds years to our life, as He did with Hezekiah; we praise Him for the promise of a resurrection unto eternal life!

Basic religious teachings of the text:

1. The imminence of death is an occasion for prayer. The content of prayer may vary (see Hezekiah and Paul), but the true believer seeks always to know and to abide in the will of God.

2. The prayer of the believer who faces death is heard by God and answered by Him in His wisdom and in His own way. The answer

given to Hezekiah may not be the answer given to us, except the assurance, "I have heard your prayer"; but whatever the answer, it will be for our good.

3. The recovery of Hezekiah was connected with the deliverance of his city (Jerusalem) out of the hand of the king of Assyria. God needed a man like Hezekiah, and the added years of life became added years of service to God and to his people. So with Paul (Philippians 1).

4. The mercy of God in saving from death is connected with His mercy in forgiving sin (vs. 17).

5. The answer to prayer leads to praise of God for His truth and faithfulness.

New Testament echoes of the text:

1. The imagery of vs. 12a is similar to that of II Corinthians 5:1, 4, and II Peter 1:13, 14. Life is compared to a dwelling, like a tabernacle or tent, which is removed or destroyed by death.

2. There is some similarity of language between verse 12b and Hebrews 1:12, though they do not refer to the same thing; the Isaiah passage refers to the manner in which death ends life, the Hebrews passage to the end of the age as it affects the heavens and the earth.

3. There is marked similarity of outlook between Hezekiah and Paul in this respect that both stress the importance of a continued ministry of praise on earth for the sake of God's people.

Seventeenth Sunday After Trinity

TOPIC FOR THE DAY: "The Liberty of the Christian."

TEXT: Isaiah 58 (especially vs. 1-9a).

THEME: A day acceptable to the Lord (or, The fast that God approves).

Relation of the text to the topic:

The New Testament examples of Christian liberty are especially those that show forth Jesus' attitude towards the sabbath. Man made rules and restrictions he ignored, but the fundamental spiritual and ethical purpose of the sabbath as set forth in the Mosaic law (Exodus 20:8-11; Deuteronomy 5:12-15) he respected. It was his custom to enter into the synagogue on the sabbath and to participate in its ministry of teaching and of prayer. In addition to this basic principle of sabbath observance, he laid down this guiding rule that "it is lawful to do good on the sabbath." Religious legalism was completely foreign to our Lord's teaching and practice. His approach to every question was spiritual and evangelical.

How completely his generation had missed the same essential emphasis in the prophets, including the 58th chapter of Isaiah! Here the prophet teaches in plain language what is the right observance of fasts as well as of the sabbath. Verses 3-5 give the picture of a wrong observance: they fasted because it pleased them rather than God; they paid much attention to ritual details such as sackcloth and ashes; but they showed no sign of moral repentance, for they combined fasting with oppression and wickedness, and the result of their religious exercises was a spirit of strife and contention rather than a spirit of peace and good will. Verses 6-7 are the picture of a right observance: "Is not this the fast that I choose: to loose the bonds of wickedness, to undo the thongs of the yoke, to let the oppressed go free, and to break every yoke? Is it not to share your bread with the hungry, and to bring the homeless poor into your house; when you see the naked, to cover him, and not to hide yourself from your own flesh?" Need it be pointed out that God is not interested in ritual exercises but in true religion; and that true religion is first of all spiritual, and then also ethical: concerned with a right relationship of the heart to God and of the life to our fellowmen. This is the liberty of the Christian, that he is not bound by rules and religious forms, but is free to serve God in righteousness and his neighbor in love.

Basic religious teachings of the text:

1. The incompatability of wickedness and worship (vs. 1, 2). See Isaiah 1:13.

2. The hypocritical pretence to righteousness and to religious piety is denounced by God; because they delighted in religious forms, but cared nothing for the spiritual and ethical requirements of God.

3. The wrong and the right observance of fasts and of the sabbath; religious formalism and legalism versus evangelical spirituality and morality.

4. The glory of the covenant relationship promised again when they learn to worship in spirit and in truth (vs. 8-9).

New Testament echoes of the text:

1. There is an obvious parallelism of thought between vs. 2 and Titus 1:16.

2. The attitude that fasting is a good work which God ought to acknowledge is like that of the Pharisee in the parable (Luke 18:12).

3. The teaching of verses 6-7 is markedly similar to that of Jesus in Matthew 25:31-46. "You will know them by their fruits."

Eighteenth Sunday After Trinity

Topic for the Day: "The Way of Perfection."

Text: Isaiah 33:13-16.

Theme: Who shall dwell with God in His holy place?

Relation of the text to the topic:

The Old Gospel text for this Sunday gives us Jesus' answer to the question, "Which is the great commandment in the law?" Another lesson gives his answer to the question of the rich young ruler, "What must I do to inherit eternal life?" There is a marked similarity between these questions, and the answers given, and the question in our text: "Who among us can dwell with the devouring fire? Who among us can dwell with everlasting burnings?" It may help us in our thinking if we include also the questions in Psalm 15:1 and Psalm 24:3, together with the answers that follow.

There are two ways in which to interpret and use all of these passages. The one is to see in them *pure Law,* whose sole purpose is to convict man of sin, in that he has not kept the law nor indeed can he keep it so as to have a righteousness of his own before God. The other is to see in them a guide to righteous living: Divine directives as to the true nature of the righteous life which God seeks for His people, and which gives evidence of a right relationship with God. The two ways should not be separated in our preaching. The way of perfection must bring conviction of sin as we realize that we do not, and cannot, measure up"; and certainly our hope of salvation cannot be based on our own righteousness. Nevertheless the way of perfection hovers before us as an Ideal, which in a measure is attainable within the covenant fellowship of God, and which testifies to the fact that we do live in that fellowship by faith.

God looks for a walk in the newness of life on the part of His people. He looks for those things of which the prophet speaks in vs. 15: "He who walks righteously and speaks uprightly; he who despises the gain of oppressions, who shakes his hands, lest they hold a bribe, who stops his ears from hearing of bloodshed, and shuts his eyes from looking upon evil." On these things God looks with favor; for this is the way of perfection in which the believer is invited, and commanded, and enabled, to walk, and these are the evidences that we are living in a right relationship with the holy God as a holy people. It is not as if the trembling sinners (vs. 14) could stand before God "on their record"; they need forgiveness, and there is forgiveness with God (see Isaiah 33:24). But sinners whose only concern is to be forgiven, and who are unconcerned about obedience to the will of God after they have been forgiven, cannot dwell with God in His holy place. Psalm 130:4 is to the point: "There is forgiveness with thee, that thou mayest be feared."

The prophetic preaching in verse 15 of our text is relevant today as indicating a significant aspect of the way of perfection for those who bear the name of Christ, and for a nation that wants to be known as a Christian nation. The reassuring promise in verse 16 is like the words of the wise man in Proverbs 14:34, "Righteousness exalts a nation"; or of the psalmist in Psalm 1:6, "For the Lord knows the way of the righteous"; or of Jesus in Matthew 5:20, when he speaks of the righteousness that exceeds that of the scribes and Pharisees. To be right with God means that we earnestly seek to live right with men: the way of salvation by faith leads to the way of perfection in life *in aim* if not always in achievement.

Basic religious teachings of the text:

1. The works of God, both judgment and redemption, should cause us to acknowledge Him and His might (vs. 13).

2. The judgments of God cause sinners to tremble and should move them to repentance (vs. 14a), for they reveal God as "the devouring fire" (vs. 14b).

3. The holiness of God demands a holy people, a people dedicated to righteousness in all human relationships (vs. 15).

4. The man or the nation that truly seeks God and His righteousness shall experience His blessing (vs. 16).

New Testament echoes of the text:

1. The concept of God as a devouring fire is found also in Hebrews 12:29.

2. The New Testament also stresses the importance of walking righteously; or, in New Testament language, of walking worthily of the calling with which we have been called. See Ephesians 4:1; Colossians 1:10; I Thessalonians 2:12.

Nineteenth Sunday After Trinity

TOPIC FOR THE DAY: "The Narrow Way of Faith."

TEXT: Isaiah 7:9b (and context).

THEME: Believe in the Lord your God, and you will be established. (II Chronicles 20:20).

Relation of the text to the topic:

The importance, and even the necessity, of faith is stressed in many of the lessons for this Sunday. The reference is not so much to the faith that is reckoned for righteousness as to the need of faith in God in all of life's experiences. When Jesus saw the faith of the men who brought to him the palsied man, he reacted to that faith by giving both physical and spiritual healing to the man who was sick. Faith led to his being "established," which is another way of saying that he was delivered out of his troubles. In every time of need faith in God is the final place of refuge and source of help.

In II Chronicles 20, at a critical moment in the history of Judah, Jehoshaphat the king was told by God's prophet Jahaziel not to fear, "for the battle is not yours but God's"; and thus encouraged Jehoshaphat said, to the people, "Hear me, Judah and inhabitants of Jerusalem! Believe in the Lord your God, and you will be established; believe his prophets, and you will succeed." That is the positive side of the truth.

The negative side is stated in our text (Isaiah 7:9b) as a warning from another prophet to another king in another time of national crisis. The historical situation was this: Judah was threatened with attack by a confederacy consisting of Syria and Ephraim. The purpose was to force Judah into an alliance with them against Assyria, the great imperial power threatening from the east. In preparation for a siege Ahaz the king went out to inspect his water supply, and the prophet Isaiah was sent to meet him there with the message that he need not fear if he would only put his trust in the Lord. But Ahaz had other plans. He would seek the help of Assyria rather than put his faith in God and be faithful to Him; and by so doing he brought on a greater danger and a worse evil than the one from which he sought to escape. It is before he takes the fatal step that the prophet warns him of the words of our text, "If you will not believe, surely you shall not be established."

It is a Divine truth that applies always and everywhere. It holds true for nations as well as for individuals. As Christians we are called to walk in the way of faith. It may sometimes seem to be a narrow way indeed; but it is nevertheless a good way, for the promise is that if we walk in it we shall be established. God's word to us is this, "Do not fear, only believe."

Basic religious teachings of the text:

1. Without a living and obedient faith in God foolish fears, and equally foolish plans, fill our hearts and minds.

2. If we have faith in God at all times we shall experience that He will strengthen, establish, and keep us in all our ways.

3. It is more important for nations to have faith in God and to be

true to Him than it is to have many and strong allies on a basis of political expediency.

New Testament echoes of the text:

There is no direct reference to Isaiah 7:9b in the New Testament; but it is in complete harmony with the New Testament teaching concerning faith in God. "Have faith in God," said Jesus (Mark 11:22); and again, "Do not fear, only believe" (Mark 5:36); and again, "If you can! All things are possible to him who believes" (Mark 9:23).

Twentieth Sunday After Trinity

TOPIC FOR THE DAY: "Spiritual Indifference."

TEXT: Isaiah 22:12-14.

THEME: "Let us eat and drink, for tomorrow we die."

Relation of the text to the topic:

There are two ways in which men may reveal an attitude of spiritual indifference. The one is by rejecting God's gracious invitation, as in Jesus' parable of the marriage feast and the slighted invitation (Matthew 22:1-14). The other is by refusing the spiritual demands of God's law, and letting a crass materialism dominate one's life instead, as in the prophecy of Isaiah which is our text for the day.

It was a time of critical danger for Judah as a nation, when foreign enemies invaded the land and threatened to destroy even Jerusalem, the city of David. In that day the Lord God of hosts called the people to repentance (vs. 12) and to prayer; but to such a plea, with all its spiritual implications, they were utterly indifferent. Instead, though danger and even death stared them in the face, they continued in revelry and self-indulgence, and seemingly justified it with a fatalistic shrug of the shoulders, saying, "Let us eat and drink, for tomorrow we die." As Paul says in I Corinthians 15:32, where he quotes this sentence, such an attitude is to be expected in one who does not believe in the resurrection of the dead, and who therefore does not acknowledge that there are spiritual and moral verities with eternal significance; but it is utterly unbecoming a believer in the living God or a people living in covenant fellowship with Him. Whether in time of prosperity or of adversity, we are tempted to forget spiritual needs and to cater to fleshly lusts; materialism crowds out spirituality. It is on such an attitude of spiritual indifference, which remains deaf to the Divine pleading, that this terrible judgment is pronounced, "Surely this iniquity will not be forgiven you till you die, says the Lord God of hosts" (vs. 14). God can do nothing for the spiritually indifferent, because their indifference becomes a spiritual roadblock in the way of His blessing. The relevance of the text in this day and age when materialism is rampant can readily be seen.

Another fitting text for this theme of spiritual indifference is Isaiah 6:9-10, which is quoted by both Jesus and Paul in explanation of the spiritual resistance to their preaching. It was in large measure the resistance of spiritual indifference.

Basic religious teachings of the text:

1. The call of God to repentance in the day of national calamity and crisis.

2. The resistance to that call in the form of materialism and self-indulgence.

3. The judgment upon this spiritual indifference, as a sin that cannot be forgiven; because the very nature of the sin is such that it makes forgiveness impossible. Only when we are roused from our spiritual apathy can God deal with us in a spiritual way.

New Testament echoes of the text:

1. The situation in verse 13 is very similiar to the one described by Jesus in Luke 17:26-29 and Matthew 24:37-39, where the days of Noah are likened to the days of the Son of man. Each situation reveals a spirit of materialism and of indifference to spiritual things.

2. Paul quotes the last clause of verse 13 in I Corinthians 15:32.

Twenty-first Sunday After Trinity

TOPIC FOR THE DAY: "The Foundation of Faith."

TEXT: Isaiah 26:1-4.

THEME: The mind stayed on Thee Thou keepest in perfect peace (vs. 3, AJV).

Relation of the text to the topic:

Faith is a tremendously vital thing in the Christian life; and it is therefore natural that it should be to the fore in the lessons for more than one Sunday in the church year. The general topic for the 19th Sunday after Trinity is "The narrow way of faith"; for today it is "The foundation of faith." If there is a difference between the lessons on faith for the two Sundays it is this, that the former emphasizes more the *necessity* of faith and the latter the *certainty* and sure foundation of faith.

The text from Isaiah 26:1-4 fits in beautifully with the latter emphasis. Faith is trust in the Lord as an everlasting rock, or a sure defence, and as the author of salvation, for His people. Faith in God gives to the mind perfect peace. Faith is a necessary prerequisite to the experience of the salvation promised by God, for it is faith that ventures out on the sure promises of God. It is "the righteous nation which keeps faith" that enters in through the gates into the city for which God has appointed salvation as walls and bulwarks. Though "keeps faith" really means "keeps faithfulness" we may say that faith is of the essence also of faithfulness and of righteousness (the righteous nation). The text may have a local reference to an earthly city such as Jerusalem, and to a temporal salvation from foreign enemies; and yet, since this nation in its historical experience was the people of God, the teaching involved is for God's people always and everywhere. The truth enunciated in vs. 3 has relevancy for every Christian who, because his mind is stayed on God and on Christ, knows the peace of God that passes all understanding. What is said of Jehovah in the Old Testament takes on new meaning as we see God revealed in Jesus, and the faith in Christ becomes the foundation of our life and the source of our peace. The New Testament clothes the concepts of salvation and of faith and of peace with a deeper and a more personal and an eternal meaning.

In language as well as in thought there is a close tie-up between the text from Isaiah and the Old Epistle text for the day (Ephesians 6:10-18.) The same is true of Isaiah 59:15b-21, which could be used as an alternate text for this Sunday; compare especially verse 17 with Ephesians 6:14, "the breastplate of righteousness," and with Ephesians 6:17, "the helmet of salvation."

Basic religious teachings of the text:

1. Salvation and security are promised for the people of the city of God.

2. The righteous nation, which keeps faith and faithfulness, shall share this salvation and security.

3. The result of trusting in God and in His salvation is perfect peace of mind in every time of trouble and need.

4. Therefore we are admonished to trust in the Lord at all times; for He is an everlasting Rock.

New Testament echoes of the text:

1. There is a marked parallelism of thought between Isaiah 26:3 and Philippians 4:6-7.

2. The admonition to trust in the Lord is echoed in the New Testament admonition to "have faith in God."

3. The concept of God as a Rock is typically Old Testament; but it is closely related to the New Testament concept of Christ as the cornerstone and sure foundation.

Twenty-second Sunday After Trinity

TOPIC FOR THE DAY: "Mutual Forgiveness."

TEXT: Isaiah 64:1-12.

THEME: Forgiven and forgiving.

Relation of the text to the topic:

It may seem that in this instance the Isaiah text selected misses the mark as far as the general topic for the day is concerned. The New Testament lessons lay stress on mutual forgiveness, or on forgiveness as

it is practised by the Christian as a part of his Christian life. The Old
Testament text is a confession of sin and a pleading prayer for mercy
and forgiveness from God for His sinful people. Yet, how closely related are not the two, God's forgiveness of which we have need, and
our willingness to forgive others when they stand in need of forgiveness from us. The connection is stated in one of the lessons in the
Augustana lectionary in these words, "and be kind to one another,
tenderhearted, forgiving one another, even as God in Christ forgave
you" (Ephesians 4:32). It should not be difficult to preach a sermon on
Isaiah 64 and end up with that note from Ephesians 4.

The Old Testament situation, of course, is that of God's people Israel,
sore afflicted for their sins and seemingly forgotten by God in their
affliction, pouring out their heart in confession of sin (vs. 6), and pleading for God's forgiveness and help on the basis of the covenant
relationship which He had instituted (our Father, vs. 8, thy people,
vs. 9). In the background is the concept of the faithfulness of God to
His covenant, which surely will not permit the covenant purpose with
His people to come to naught. The prayer and confession of Israel should
be ours also. The truth that "if we confess our sins, he is faithful and
just, and will forgive our sins" is seen also here, if only in the hope
and prayer of His people.

The fruit of such an experience of Divine forgiveness is a forgiving
spirit. That is not stated in the text, but it is certainly suggested by
it; for when God forgives us He expects us to be merciful. That was
the very nature of the covenant relationship from the beginning. It may
well be that the very lack of this forgiving spirit and of this love of
"hesed" (kindness, mercy) which the prophet Micah said was one of
three fundamental requirements of God (Micah 6:8) had contributed
to bringing on the present afflictions, and that it is included in their
confession of sins. It certainly ought to be included! A people living in
covenant fellowship with the Lord, who is "a God merciful and gracious, slow to anger, and abounding in steadfast love and faithfulness,
keeping steadfast love for thousands, forgiving iniquity and transgression and sin" (Exodus 34:6, 7), must surely be expected to share
His spirit. That is what Jesus meant when He said, "he who is
forgiven little, loves little" (Luke 7:47).

Basic religious teachings of the text:

1. The functional theology of verse 4: a God "who works for those who wait for Him."

2. The thoroughgoing confession of sin in verse 6, and the related thought of judgment (we fade like a leaf, our iniquities take us away).

3. The acknowledgment that penitent prayer and confident faith have all too long been lacking (vs. 7).

4. The acknowledgment of God as "our Father" and as "our potter," with Israel as His people, and the work of His hand (vs. 8, 9); reminiscent of the covenant with Abraham.

5. The prayer in verses 9-12, showing concern for God's glory as well as for personal need.

New Testament echoes of the text:

1. I Corinthians 2:9 has language similar to that of Isaiah 64:4. If a quotation, it is freely rendered, and applied to a new situation.

2. The concept of the potter appears also in Romans 9:20-21, in relation to Israel as well as the Gentiles.

3. The concept of "our Father" as used here is typically Old Testament, but it is not unrelated to the more clearly developed New Testament concept of the Fatherhood of God.

Twenty-third Sunday After Trinity

TOPIC FOR THE DAY: "Christian Patriotism."

TEXT: Isaiah 30:1-2 and 31:1-3.

THEME: The folly of trusting in men instead of in God.

Relation of the text to the topic:

Another way of stating the theme of the lessons for this Sunday is "the duty of citizenship in the Christian life." We have a duty as Christians over against the State, as citizens of a country whose privileges we enjoy. There is a higher citizenship also, for the Christian says with Paul, "Our commonwealth is in heaven" (Philippians 3:20); but this heavenly citizenship does not nullify my American citizenship on earth.

What is my duty as a Christian citizen in relation to my country and my government? Some of the answers given in the lessons for the day are these: to pay my share of the taxes required for the functioning of the State, to pray for those in authority that they may lead us in safe and peaceful and righteous paths, to be in subjection to rightful government as unto a power ordained of God, to honor and respect those to whom authority is entrusted, to live law-abiding lives that respect the rights of others (see the Golden Rule, Matthew 7:12). To these we could add many more. The prophets would add the duty of the citizen to point out what is right and wrong in our national policies, so as to influence our leaders to lead in the right direction.

In Isaiah 30 and 31 the children of Judah and their leaders are called "rebellious children" because, in a time of national crisis, they put their trust in a league with Egypt rather than in knowing and doing the will of God. They trusted in human might, in weapons of war (chariots and horsemen), instead of looking to God and seeking what was right in the sight of the Holy One of Israel. They paid more attention to military than to spiritual armaments; and they made a mistake in so doing. Any nation that neglects the spiritual and ethical laws of God and trusts solely in armaments and in alliances for self-preservation and protection is making a sad mistake; and it is the duty of the Christian citizen to point out the mistake and to try to rectify it by putting the primary emphasis in national life where it belongs, on faith in God and on righteousness in the community at every level. It may be necessary sometimes for a nation to fight to protect itself, but if we are to be sure of victory we need more than atomic weapons, however deadly and fearful their power: we need to be sure that we are on the side of God and of right in all our national aspirations and policies. Militarism is a poor excuse for righteousness as a means to establish and exalt a nation. See Isaiah 30:15.

Basic religious teachings of the text:

1. The folly of a national policy that does not consult God's Holy Spirit for guidance in its formulation.

2. The folly of trusting in an alliance with Egypt (any nation), since

the Egyptians are men, and not God, in spite of their boasted military power.

3. The power of God to cause both the one that helps and the one that is helped in military ventures to stumble and fall and to be consumed.

New Testament echoes of the text:

1. Isaiah says of God that "he is wise" (Isaiah 31:2). Paul says of Him that He is "the only wise God" (Romans 16:27).

2. The tendency of rulers to arrogate unto themselves the claim to God-likeness is seen in the Old Testament, in the New Testament, and in secular history of our own day. See Ezekiel 28:9 and II Thessalonians 2:4 (the anti-christ).

3. The situation in Isaiah 31:3, Egypt helping Judah, and both stumbling and falling, is similar to the case described by Jesus where the blind lead the blind, and both fall into the ditch (Matthew 15:14).

Twenty-fourth Sunday After Trinity

TOPIC FOR THE DAY: "The Life That Never Dies."

TEXT: Isaiah 60:15-22.

THEME: The Lord will be your everlasting light.

Relation of the text to the topic:

Some of the New Testament lessons for this Sunday speak of the resurrection and others of eternal life, or of the inheritance of the saints in light (Colossians 1:12). A good text, therefore, would be Isaiah 25: 6-8 (see Easter Sunday). The prophetic declaration, "He will swallow up death forever, and the Lord God will wipe away tears from all faces, and the reproach of his people he will take away from all the earth," sounds like it might have been taken from the book of Revelation. The text that we have chosen, however, is from Isaiah 60:15-22. The entire 60th chapter is a description of the glorified Zion of the future; and in the description are blended colors from history and from eschatology, and from heaven and earth.

It is not always easy to interpret such a prophecy so as to give due emphasis to each element in the picture. In the prophecy before us it seems quite evident that chronology is not as important as content. Starting with Zion's present affliction, which may refer to Israel's experience of captivity at the hands of her enemies, the prophecy focuses on the day when God shall remove her affliction and shall exalt His people, and shall accomplish upon them all the blessings at which His covenant with them aimed. It is this picture of the Ideal future of Zion that seems to transcend the bounds of time and to project into eternity. The statement, "the Lord will be your everlasting light, and your God will be your glory," could indeed have a spiritual meaning for Israel here on earth; but it seems to include more. Even as the everlasting covenant of blessing with Abraham found its ultimate fulfilment in Christ, and even as the ministry of Christ unites, as it were, earth and heaven, so also the "everlasting light" seems too glorious a concept to be limited to this earth. The language and viewpoint of verse 19 is essentially the same as in Revelation 21:23 and 22:5, except that the prophet still uses some of the "times-coloring" of the Old Testament (see verse 21).

Both the book of Isaiah and the book of Revelation point to a time of consummation of God's redemptive purpose, when the covenant promise of His gracious presence shall be fully realized and the mourning of His people shall be forever ended. That would seem to belong not only to "the latter days" but to "eternity," and therefore to include "the life that never dies," life eternal. Isaiah 60:20 and Revelation 21:4 point in the same direction and express the same hope. Both start with the truth of the presence of God in the midst of His people as the source of their light and joy and righteousness and salvation, and to the very real experience of this presence now by faith they add the hope and the promise of an experience in fullest measure hereafter and "forever." Isaiah 60 makes a good text for the preaching of the Christian hope.

Basic religious teachings of the text:

1. The forsaken and hated by men shall become an eternal excellency in God's good time. Present sorrow on the part of God's people shall be exchanged for joy.

2. The One who will work this change is the Lord, who is a Saviour and a Redeemer not only for Jacob but for the world.

3. The goal of God's redemptive work in human history is Salvation, and it leads to Praise, or to the glorification of God.

4. The concept of the Lord as an everlasting light.

5. The glorious future of God's people, when their mourning is ended and they receive their eternal inheritance.

6. The assurance of God: "I am the Lord; in its time I will hasten it."

New Testament echoes of the text:

1. The Beatitude in Matthew 5:10 (see also vs. 11-12 teaches the same reversal of fortune as Isaiah 60:15. So does Romans 8:18, and context.

2. The concept of the Lord (Jehovah) as Saviour and Redeemer is in the New Testament transferred to Christ, although in a number of instances God is also called Saviour.

3. The parallelism already noted between Isaiah 60:19-20 and Revelation 21:23 and 22:5 with reference to God as our eternal light.

4. The parallelism between Isaiah 60:20 and Revelation 21:4 with reference to the cessation of mourning.

5. The concept of inheritance (vs. 21) is spiritualized and repeated in the New Testament. See I Peter 1:3-5; Acts 20:32; Romans 8:17; Colossians 3:24.

Twenty-fifth Sunday After Trinity

Topic for the Day: "The Last Times."

Text: Isaiah 2:12-22.

Theme: There shall be a day of the Lord of hosts.

Relation of the text to the topic:

"The last times" is a Biblical concept that may suggest any one of several things: final judgment, final redemption, waiting in faith for the

coming of the Lord, the false security of unbelievers, the rising fury of
persecution against the people of God, the siren voices of false prophets
and false Christs. Each of these can be found somewhere in the lessons
for this Sunday, and a complete picture of "the last times" should include all of them. However, just as a single text may stress only one of
these truths related to the last times, so we may concentrate on only
one of them in any single sermon. The Old Testament concept of "the
day of the Lord" as seen in Isaiah 2:12-22 has relevance for the New
Testament concept of "the last times," 1st, because of its judgment
message; 2nd, because of the spirit of pride and haughtiness of men
which must be brought low; 3rd, because of the fear inspired, and the
flight attempted "from before the terror of the Lord, and from the glory
of his majesty, when he rises to terrify the earth" (vs. 21b); and 4th,
because "the Lord alone will be exalted in that day" (vs. 17b).

The Old Testament "day of the Lord" is essentially a day of judgment, but it leads to the exaltation of God and to the establishing of
His righteous rule. It may therefore be seen to precede the final coming
of His kingdom. However, as pictured by the prophets, the day of the
Lord is often seen as coming in the immediate or near future, in the
form of some great calamity such as an unprecedented locust plague
(Joel), or invasion and conquest by a foreign enemy (Zephaniah). It is
seen as coming upon the nations that were Israel's enemies and oppressors, but also upon Israel itself, or wherever a nation is ripe for
judgment. It witnesses, therefore, to the truth that God is actively engaged in righteous judgments upon men and nations *now*, in the course
of human history; but there is also an eschatological aspect to it which
seems to point to "the last times"; for it is frequently followed by a
prophetic picture of the Ideal future, when God's people shall be saved,
and the eternal kingdom of God shall have come, and God reigns alone.
It was not given to the prophets to see the times and the seasons in
historical and chronological detail. They did see with unerring spiritual
insight both the judgment motif and the redemption motif in God's
dealings with men. According to the prophets God is active in judgment and He is active redemptively *now*, in human history. The *present*
must be interpreted in the light of this double activity of God; and so
also the *future:* for the prophets predicted a day when God shall have
accomplished His work, "and the kingdom shall be the Lord's" (Oba-

diah 21). With this eschatological aspect of the day of the Lord in mind the appropriateness of Isaiah 2:12-22 as a text for this Sunday becomes apparent.

Basic religious teachings of the text:

1. The concept of sin as basically pride; a frequent note in the book of Isaiah.

2. The prediction of a day when all human pride shall be brought low, and the Lord alone shall be exalted.

3. The helplessness and fear of men in that day, if they have trusted in anyone or anything else than the Lord.

4. The cosmological power of God, who once created the earth and is capable of shaking it mightily in judgment if and when He chooses (vs. 19, 21, ASV).

5. The insignificance of man; see verse 22 in AJV: "Cease ye from man, in whose nostrils is a breath; for how little is he to be accounted!"

New Testament echoes of the text:

1. The concept of a day of judgment preliminary to the final exaltation of God and to the victory of His kingdom is as prominent in the New Testament as it is in the Old Testament.

2. The insignificance of man is described in James 4:14 in terms very similar to Isaiah 2:22.

Twenty-sixth Sunday After Trinity

TOPIC FOR THE DAY: "Watchfulness" (or, "Watchful Waiting.")

TEXT: Isaiah 65:17-25 (or Isaiah 26:8-10).

THEME: I create new heavens and a new earth.

Relation of the text to the topic:

In order to make room for as many as twenty-seven Sundays in the Trinity season of the church year Easter must come at the earliest possible date. This happens but rarely, though it did happen in 1951 when Easter came on March 25. In the Swedish Church the last Sunday before Advent is referred to as Judgment Sunday, when the lessons for the Twenty-seventh Sunday after Trinity are used because these lessons center around the theme of "The Last Judgment." That means that the lessons for the Twenty-sixth Sunday after Trinity, and sometimes also for the two preceding Sundays, are omitted in favor of the judgment texts with which the Trinity cycle closes. The result is that the texts for the Twenty-sixth Sunday after Trinity, which are the same as those for the Sixth Sunday after Epiphany, are very seldom used. (The ELC lectionary lists the same texts for the Sixth Sunday after Epiphany and the Twenty-seventh Sunday after Trinity.) A few of the texts for the Twenty-sixth Sunday after Trinity, but not all of them, deal with the theme of the last judgment.

Under the circumstances it may seem relatively unimportant what text if any is selected from Isaiah for this Sunday. The choice of Isaiah 65:17-25 is motivated by a striking thought-relationship with II Peter 3:3-13, the first Epistle in the Augustana lectionary. "For behold, I create new heavens and a new earth" is the prediction and promise in Isaiah 65:17; and to this II Peter 3:13 responds, "But according to his promise we wait for new heavens and a new earth in which righteousness dwells." The attitude of watchful waiting and of holy living is stressed in the Epistle as the only right attitude while we look for the fulfilment of the promise given in the Old Testament prophecy. The very nature of the prophecy is such as to inspire the forward look of faith and hope. When Jesus said, "Heaven and earth shall pass away, but my words shall not pass away," he too seems to have been looking forward to new heavens and a new earth to take the place of those that will pass away. Whether this "newness" is to be physically or spiritually construed, or perhaps as a blending of both, may have to await the fulfilment to determine; certainly the spiritual renewal cannot be omitted from the promise. Peter's emphasis on righteousness makes that clear.

Another text that stresses the theme of waiting for the Lord in time of tribulation is Isaiah 26:8-10. The attitude indicated in verse 8a, "In the path of thy judgments, O Lord, we wait for thee," and the significant statement in verse 9b, "for when thy judgments are in the earth, the inhabitants of the world learn righteousness," have relevance for us as we draw nearer to that day of cataclysmic judgments and changes which shall usher in the new heavens and the new earth wherein righteousness dwells, and also peace and everlasting joy (see again Isaiah 65:17-25).

Basic religious teachings of the text (Isaiah 65:17-25):

1. The stupendous concept of new heavens and a new earth, or a new creation: a concept wherein the spiritual and religious seems to blend with the physical or material. The picture reflects the Creation chapter of Genesis, and also the covenant with Abraham and with Israel, and looks forward to a glorious goal.

2. The joy that awaits God's people because of God's joy in His people: "be glad and rejoice—for behold, I create Jerusalem a rejoicing, and her people a joy" (vs. 18).

3. The Ideal future, pictured for us in colors borrowed from this earth, but pointing always to the new heavens and the new earth: no more weeping, length of days, undisturbed prosperity, no more labor in vain, God so near that He answers before they call, peace as in the original Paradise, none to hurt or destroy; Paradise on earth, the new earth.

4. The wonderful assurance in verse 24. We know Him now as a prayer-answering God; but oh, what shall it be like then, when He anticipates even the prayer, and answers before we get done praying!

Basic religious teachings of the text (Isaiah 26:8-10).

1. When God's judgments come upon us in this life the true believer waits for the Lord to save.

2. When God's judgments are in the earth the inhabitants of the world learn righteousness, whereas if favor be shown to the wicked he continues in his wickedness and fails to see the glory of God.

New Testament echoes of the text:

1. The promise of new heavens and a new earth in Isaiah 65:17 becomes in II Peter 3:13 the motivation for faith and hope. See also the book of Revelation.

2. The prediction in Isaiah 65:19 that there shall be no more weeping is paralleled by the more extended statements in Revelation 7:17 and 21:4.

148

Twenty-seventh Sunday After Trinity

TOPIC FOR THE DAY: "The Last Judgment."

TEXT: Isaiah 66:15-24.

THEME: For by fire will the Lord execute judgment.

Relation of the text to the topic:

The prophecy in Isaiah 66:15-24 is right in line with the texts for Judgment Sunday. There is a finality and a universality about it that makes it clear that it belongs to the time of the end, as the final chapter in God's judgment-redemption activity. We say this in spite of the fact that there are also many things in the prophecy that reflect the "times-coloring" of the Old Testament and of the national experience of the people of Israel. The concept of judgment by fire is the pictorial counterpart of the concept of God as a devouring fire (see Isaiah 33: 14). The fact that the judgment is executed *upon all flesh* is one indication of its universality and finality. The reference in verse 17 to a peculiar instance of idolatrous abomination is a part of the local "times-coloring" through which the prophecy looks forward. It may stand as a symbol of all rejection of the living covenant God of Israel. The gathering of all nations to see God's glory seems to point to the conversion of the Gentiles, as they also are brought into the covenant of blessing with Abraham which was to be mediated to the world by Israel as a kingdom of priests. The bringing of all the children of Israel from their far-flung dispersion, and the emphasis on "my holy mountain Jerusalem," reflect the Old Testament "times-coloring" once more; but they seem to point to a grander, more spiritual return than from a purely earthly captivity: what is visualized is the complete and permanent realization of everything that God's covenant with Israel stood for. It seems that the whole covenant concept is so spiritualized in outlook that even the Old Testament priesthood gives place to a more universal priesthood (see verse 21), which may be related to the New Testament concept of the priesthood of all believers. The picture of the new heavens and the new earth which we meet here again (see chapter 65) is still presented in terms of *time* and *space* and of repeated rather than continual experiences of worship; but in spite of these limitations in the terminology employed, the eternal spiritual realities that they represent seem unmistakable. This is not a halfway stop but the final goal of the kingdom of God, only seen through the "times-coloring" of the Old Testament. The New Testament removes the "times-coloring" but points to the same goal. After the last judgment is finished, God will reach His redemptive and covenant goal in the new heavens and the new earth of His own creating, with a spiritually reborn people from out of all nations as His new creation.

Basic religious teachings of the text:

1. The execution of Divine judgment with the devastating power of flames of fire and of the whirlwind.

2. The gathering of all nations to see the glory of the Lord as the God of redemption and of judgment.

3. The universal priesthood implied in verse 21, in fulfilment of the calling of Israel to be "a kingdom of priests," and in harmony with the frequent prophetic concept that *all things* shall be "Holy to the Lord" (Zechariah 14:20-21).

4. The new heavens and the new earth which shall abide before God.

5. The universal and continuing worship before the Lord.

New Testament echoes of the text:

1. Many of the concepts enumerated above are found also in the New Testament, though stated in different language.

2. The reference in I Peter 2:5, 9, to a *holy* and a *royal* priesthood which includes every Christian may reflect the teaching of Isaiah 66:21 as well as of Exodus 19:6.

3. The new heavens and the new earth which shall remain (Isaiah 66:22) remind of Hebrews 12:26-27.

4. The concept of the new heavens and the new earth is met again in II Peter 3:13 and in Revelation 21:1.

5. Jesus as well as Isaiah refers to the worm that does not die; see Mark 9:48.

6. John the Baptist as well as Isaiah speaks of an unquenchable fire; see Matthew 3:12.

Minor Festivals of the Church Year

In his discussion of the church year, in his book "Grunden," Bo Giertz includes five "holy days" which occur at a fixed time during the year. These are also listed in the Augustana lectionary under the heading "Minor Festivals of the Church Year." They are the Day of the Presentation of Christ (or Candlemas), the Day of Annunciation, the Day of John the Baptist, St. Michael's Day, and All Saints' Day. Although these Minor Festivals are not uniformly observed in the Lutheran Churches of America, they do represent incidents or truths that have sufficient significance for the Christian life to warrant their inclusion here.

The Day of the Presentation of Christ

(Candlemas)

TOPIC FOR THE DAY: "The Presentation of Christ in the Temple."
TEXT: Isaiah 49:5-6.
THEME: I will give you as a light to the nations.

Relation of the text to the topic:

It might be more correct to call this day the day of the Purification of Mary, the mother of Jesus; for the story in Luke 2:22-32 records the faithful obedience to the command in Leviticus 12 concerning the purification of women after childbirth. This took place on the 40th day after birth in the case of a male child. There is nothing in the Levitical law as to the presentation of the child to the Lord *at this same time;* but there is the command in Exodus 13:2, 12, as to the sanctification of every firstborn male unto the Lord, with nothing said as to the time or as to any official ceremony with which it was to be observed. In the time of our Lord the purification of the mother and the presentation of the child were evidently observed by faithful Israelites at one and the same time. The narrative in Luke, however, focuses attention chiefly on the child, and on his presentation to the Lord. There is involved the element of *consecration* or of *dedication* of the child to the Lord. The closing part of Simeon's song, the Nunc Dimittis, comes like an echo of faith to the servant-prophecy in Isaiah 49:5-6; and the song as well as the prophecy emphasizes *the function* of the Messiah as the servant of God and the bringer of salvation unto the end of the earth. The Old Testament rite of presentation implied consecration unto God in holy service; the same theme of consecration of God's service is stressed by the prophet with respect to the servant; and Simeon takes up the theme and applies it to Jesus.

Other lessons for the day stress the concept of light and of revelation, the Epiphany theme. In that connection it is interesting to note that Candlemas, as the festival is more familiarly called, is observed about the first of February and would therefore usually come within the Epiphany season. A similar servant-prophecy, Isaiah 42:1-7, was used as the text for the Sunday after New Year. It could have been used here. Another appropriate text would be Isaiah 52:7-10, whose language is reflected not only in Simeon's song ("mine eyes have seen thy salvation") but also in the story of Anna that follows it ("the redemption of Jerusalem"). See the Fourth Sunday in Lent.

Basic religious teachings of the text:

1. The consecration of the servant from the womb to a Divinely appointed task.

2. The personal nature of the servant, who is charged with a mission to both Israel and the Gentiles.

3. The servant as a representative of God ("my servant," "my salvation").

4. The universal scope of the servant's mission, to bring salvation to the end of the earth.

New Testament echoes of the text:

1. Paul quotes Isaiah 49:6b in Acts 15:47 in justification of his ministry to the Gentiles.

2. The double aspect of the servant's work, in relation to Jews and to Gentiles, is reflected in the words of Simeon (Luke 2:32). So also "my salvation" in Isaiah 49:6 becomes "thy salvation" in Luke 2:30.

The Day of Annunciation

TOPIC FOR THE DAY: "The Announcement of the Incarnation."

TEXT: Isaiah 7:10-15 or Isaiah 49:5-6.

THEME: Immanuel promised.

Relation of the text to the topic:

The Day of Annunciation is celebrated on March 25. The Augustana lectionary includes the two lessons from Isaiah listed above. The Immanuel prophecy is a natural text for this festival, just as it is for New Year's Day. The servant prophecy fits in equally well on the day of Annunciation or on the day of the Presentation of Christ, because of its Messianic significance. Since the festival of the Annunciation usually falls on a weekday rather than on a Sunday it is not observed as often as most other festivals. We content ourselves with listing the two texts that could be used if the day were celebrated.

The Day of John the Baptist

TOPIC FOR THE DAY: "The Ministry of John."

TEXT: Isaiah 40:1-8 or Isaiah 61:7-11.

THEME: The announcement of blessings to come.

Relation of the text to the topic:

This festival is celebrated on the 24th of June, which is Midsummer Day. The lessons center around the birth, life, and death of John the Baptist. The first Epistle in the Augustana lectionary is Isaiah 40:1-8; a natural selection since, according to Luke 3:1-6, a portion of the prophecy found fulfilment in the ministry of John. We have used the same text for the Third Sunday in Advent: see analysis there. Another appropriate text for this day is Isaiah 61:7-11. There is no direct reference either to the herald or to the Messiah; but the day of which it speaks, the day of Zion's future glory, would seem to be the day that was ushered in by the Christ, whose herald was John. A careful comparison of the Benedictus in Luke 1:67-79 with Isaiah 61:7-11 will show that they have many things in common: references to the covenant, to the seed of Abraham which God has blessed, to salvation, to righteousness, to joy and peace. The statement in verse 8, "For I the Lord love justice, I hate robbery and wrong," certainly resembles the preaching of repentance and of righteousness by John the Baptist. The seventh verse is closely related in thought to Isaiah 40:1-2. Both Isaiah passages mentioned as possible texts for the day predict a fulfilment of God's covenant purpose with His people; and as the prophecy was translated into history the significant role of both the herald and of the Messianic king in connection with the fulfilment becomes clear.

Basic religious teachings of the text:

1. The promise of everlasting joy to God's people after they have been chastened for a while for their sins.

2. The promise of an everlasting covenant based on justice and truth (faithfulness).

3. The fulfilment of the promise of blessing to Abraham in his seed, "a people whom the Lord has blessed."

4. The rejoicing of God's people in their God and in His salvation.

5. The clothing of God's people in the garments of salvation and of righteousness.

6. The prediction that the Lord will cause righteousness and praise to spring forth before all the nations through His redeemed people.

New Testament echoes of the text:

The similarity with the Benedictus in Luke 1 has already been noted. Each item in the list is a Biblical truth which is found with equal frequency in the Old Testament and in the New, with the deep spiritual character of each concept more clearly seen in the New.

154

St. Michael's Day

TOPIC FOR THE DAY: "Greatness and Lowliness."

TEXT: Isaiah 57:15-16.

THEME: God dwells with him who is of a contrite and humble spirit.

Relation of the text to the topic:

This festive day is celebrated on the first of October, or on a Sunday near to it. The lessons for the day emphasize the place of little children in relation to the kingdom of heaven; and from this point of view it is fitting that the date set for its observance is at the time of the year when many churches observe Sunday School Rally and Promotion Day. However, the real theme of the day is to be found in Jesus' answer to the question of his disciples, "Who is the greatest in the kingdom of heaven?" (Matthew 18:1-10). Using a little child as an object-lesson, Jesus stressed that in order to be truly great in the kingdom of heaven we must humble ourselves and become as little children. Genuine faith is always humble and teachable, and ready to receive what God gives, both in the way of teaching and of salvation.

It is this same attitude that is referred to in our Isaiah text as a contrite and humble spirit. Isaiah 57:15 is one of the grandest statements in all Scripture: God, "the high and lofty one who inhabits eternity" and "whose name is Holy" declares that He will dwell "with him who is of a contrite and humble spirit," in order "to revive" the fainting spirit of men whom He himself has made. It is a marvelous declaration of God's grace; but it is an equally significant declaration of His approval of a contrite and humble heart. Such a one He will exalt by His presence and with His gracious help. Another fine reference to this same spirit is found in Isaiah 66:2, "But this is the man to whom I will look, he that is humble and contrite in spirit, and trembles at my word."

Basic religious teachings of the text:

1. The exalted theology: the glory and holiness of God, who inhabits eternity; the condescending grace and mercy of God, who stoops to help the meek and lowly in his need.

2. The glorious assurance for him who is humble and contrite in

heart: God is willing to dwell with him, and to let him live in fellowship with Himself.

3. The purpose of God's dwelling among (with) men, as envisioned in the original covenant with Abraham and with Israel and fulfilled in the new covenant in Jesus' blood, is to revive hearts that otherwise would faint "beneath life's crushing load."

New Testament echoes of the text:

1. The Beatitude, "Blessed are the poor in spirit, for theirs is the kingdom of heaven," reflects the same spirit as Isaiah 57:15.

2. The statement of Jesus that "he who humbles himself will be exalted" (Luke 18:14) is also in line with the teaching of Isaiah 57:15-16.

3. The concept of God as *Holy* is echoed by Jesus when he called God "Holy Father" (John 17:11).

4. The description of God given by Paul in I Timothy 6:15, 16, is markedly similar in grandeur to that in Isaiah 57:15.

All Saints' Day

Topic for the Day: "The Saints."

Text: Isaiah 56:1-5.

Theme: The present and the future of the people of God.

Relation of the text to the topic:

There is an interesting and significant combination of viewpoints in the lessons for All Saints' Day. The Epistle lessons are primarily concerned with the eternal aspect of the experience of God's people, in heaven with God; while the Gospel lessons speak more of their present function to be a salt and a light among men on earth. Included among the lessons for the day are the Beatitudes (Matthew 5) and the prophetic picture of the great white host (Revelation 7). Two things, therefore, come in for emphasis: the present duty of God's people, who according to the New Testament are called saints, to glorify God by living worthily of their high calling; and the glorious future hope for God's people, when they shall know everlasting peace and joy.

It is possible to duplicate each of these two teachings from the book of Isaiah.

A surprisingly large number of prophecies speak of the day when God will wipe away tears from all faces (25:8); when the people of Zion shall weep no more (30:19); when sorrow and sighing shall flee away (35:10 and 51:11); when the days of mourning shall be ended (60:20); when the anointed of the Lord shall comfort them who mourn (61:1-3); and when the sound of weeping and the cry of distress shall be heard no more (65:19). Any one of these prophecies would make a good All Saints' Day text. Though the "times-coloring" of the covenant with Israel is evident, there is an eschatological and a spiritual outlook which definitely transcends that covenant in its national phase, and which focuses our attention on the same ultimate goal as do the Revelation-pictures with a similar message of hope.

The book of Isaiah also stresses frequently that the life of God's people here on earth should be in conformity with its covenant faith. The two key-notes in this message are justice and righteousness (see Isaiah 5:7; 33:5; 56:1). Matthew 5, from which two of the Gospel lessons for the day are taken, also lays strong emphasis on righteousness of life as a fruit and evidence of faith. One might even find three "Beatitudes" in Isaiah which resemble those in Matthew 5: see Isaiah 30:18; 32:20; 56:2.

The text that we have selected from the wealth of available material is Isaiah 56:1-5. It combines in one text the admonition to live worthily of our calling ("keep justice, and do righteousness"), the promise of a brighter future day ("for soon my salvation will come") which shall include all men ("the foreigner," "the eunuch"), the declaration that the man who does this (keeps the covenant, of which the sabbath was a sign) is blessed, and the assurance of an everlasting name better than that of sons and daughters, within the spiritual household of God. While some of these things belong to the experience of God's people on earth, and some even reflect the spiritual and historical milieu of the old covenant with Israel as a nation, there is a depth and a breadth to the prophecy that seems to link it with the Ideal future and the consummation of the covenant with Israel; and that has relevance for the Christian faith, life, and hope of them who in the New Testament are called "saints."

Basic religious teachings of the text:

1. God's people should keep justice and do righteousness, for such is the spirit of the covenant whose privileges they enjoy.

2. The declaration, "for soon my salvation will come, and my deliverance be revealed," points to a brighter day for God's people, who are also called His servants and His saints.

3. The Beatitude in verse 2 is pronounced as a benediction on those who live in faithfulness to the covenant relationship with God.

4. The universality of the covenant in its ultimate fulfilment is indicated.

5. The "eternal" aspect of the prophecy, and of the original covenant to whose fulfilment it points, is suggested by the *everlasting name* better than the name of sons and daughters.

New Testament echoes of the text:

There is no direct quotation from it in the New Testament. The concepts listed above are a part of New Testament teaching also.

First Day of Prayer

TOPIC FOR THE DAY: "Repentance."

TEXT: Isaiah 59:1-15a (or the whole chapter).

THEME: A confession of national wickedness.

Relation of the text to the topic:

This chapter from Isaiah makes a perfect text for a national day of Penitence and Prayer. It concerns God's Old Testament people Israel, but it contains truths that can be applied to any nation. The sequence within the chapter is significant: 1st, the prophetic indictment of the sinful situation that prevailed (vs. 1-8); 2nd, the public confession of sin as being the cause of the judgment that was upon them (vs. 9-15a); and 3rd, the Divine promise of the coming of a Redeemer to deliver them that turn from transgression (vs. 15b-21). There are repeated references to "iniquity" in the chapter. The description of the national wickedness is vivid in the extreme. Especially significant are the prophet's spiritual interpretation of the present situation (vs. 1-2) and the penitent people's confession of the same tragic situation (vs. 12-15a), a confession of sin on the national level that sees things in all their awful reality. Underlying the whole is the concept of the Divine covenant to which He is faithful: He Himself will come as a Redeemer and will renew His covenant with His redeemed. Again we see the *goal* of the covenant, even a new covenant in the sense in which Jeremiah speaks of it (Jeremiah 31:31-34), shining through the "times-coloring" of the immediate historical situation with a promise of redemption that is basically spiritual, because it is for them that turn from transgression, and also truly Messianic, for the Redeemer who came *is* none other than the Lord Jesus Christ.

The chapter must be interpreted in the light of covenant theology; see Exodus 34:5-7. It must also be interpreted in the light of covenant eschatology. The statement in I John 1:9 summarizes the truth taught also in this chapter of Isaiah. Such was, and is, God's gracious way of dealing with transgressors who repent, be they individuals or nations. Confession of sin leads to salvation from sin. But there must be sincere confession; for if we pretend that we have not sinned we make God a liar (I John 1:8, 10), and on that basis covenant fellowship and salvation from sin and deliverance from evil of every sort cannot be enjoyed.

Basic religious teachings of the text:

It is unrepented sin that separates from God so that He will not hear our prayers.

2. The national sins of Israel are our national sins: violence and bloodshed, treachery and deceit, crooked paths instead of the way of peace, neglect of the guiding principles of righteousness, justice and truth.

3. There is no peace, says our God, to the wicked.

4. The responsibility of each citizen for the conduct of the whole nation leads naturally to the confession that "we" have sinned.

5. True confession of sin is thorough-going, holding back nothing, and also clear-sighted, recognizing transgression against both God and man. (See vs. 12-15.)

6. Basic prerequisites in a national life that has God's approval upon it are justice, righteousness, truth, and uprightness.

7. Any spiritual or ethical redemption requires the initiative of the covenant-faithful God, and the activity of the Redeemer who came in accordance with the covenant promise to save his people from their sins.

New Testament echoes of the text:

1. Verses 7 and 8 are quoted in free translation in Romans 3:15-17 as a part of the "mosaic" which includes also parts of several psalms.

2. The reference in verse 7 to "their thoughts" as the source of evil deeds corresponds with Jesus' teaching in Mark 7:21-23.

3. The phrase, "the way of peace" (vs. 8), is found in another setting in Luke 1:79.

4. The confession that they were guilty of "denying the Lord" (vs. 13) reminds of similar language in Matthew 10:33 and Titus 1:16.

5. "The breastplate of righteousness" (Ephesians 6:14) and "the helmet of salvation" (Ephesians 6:17) are reminiscent of Isaiah 59:17.

6. Paul quotes verses 20-21 with characteristic freedom as to the letter in Romans 11:26-27.

Second Day of Prayer

TOPIC FOR THE DAY: "The Reformation."

TEXT: Isaiah 26:12-13.

THEME: O Lord our God, other lords besides Thee have ruled over us.

Relation of the text to the topic:

The Reformation theme might be said to be the Rediscovery of the Gospel. The Reformation Epistle is the familiar statement of Paul in Romans 1:16-17, "I am not ashamed of the gospel." The Reformation Gospel is the equally familiar invitation of Jesus in Matthew 11:25-30, "Come to me." In line with this theme any one of the several "good tidings" passages in Isaiah would make a good Reformation text; see Isaiah 40:9; 52:7 (see quotation in Romans 10:15); and 61:1. So would passages referring to the word of God, such as Isaiah 8:16, 20, and 55:6-11; and also passages that speak of faith, such as Isaiah 7:9b and 30:15.

On the other hand, there is no passage in Isaiah that speaks specifically
of a religious reformation such as took place under Hezekiah, and later
under Josiah. In Isaiah 26:13 there is indicated an attitude that belongs
to a true reformation; for it is when we come to realize that we have
been serving other lords than the living God, and resolve from henceforth to acknowledge His name alone, that reformation results. It may
be a spiritual reformation of the individual or an ecclesiastical reformation of the whole church, but the motivating spirit is ever the same;
and this verse states it excellently. It does not lessen the value of the
text if we link it with verse 12, with its emphasis on *peace* as something
that God will ordain for us when we do acknowledge His name.

Basic religious teachings of the text:

1. The confession of the sinful mistake of having served other lords
than the Lord our God.

2. The commitment to acknowledge only the name of the Lord our
God from henceforth.

3. The assurance of a peace ordained of God for them that seek Him
in truth.

New Testament echoes of the text:

There is no direct reference to it, but the New Testament does speak
of *other lords* as well as of *the true Lord.*

Third Day of Prayer

TOPIC FOR THE DAY: "Missions."

TEXT: Isaiah 19:19-25.

THEME: And the Egyptians will know the Lord.

Relation of the text to the topic:

The Gospel for this Day of Prayer is the Great Commission in
Matthew 28:18-20, with its emphasis on making disciples of *all nations.*

There are many appropriate missionary texts in the book of Isaiah that stress the universality of the covenant purpose, which historically is equivalent to the universality of the gospel. One such passage is Isaiah 2:2-4, the text we have assigned to Epiphany. Other references to the ultimate inclusion of "all nations" within the covenant are found in Isaiah 56:7; 45:22-23; and 66:18.

The text selected predicts the day when Egypt and Assyria, both ancient enemies and oppressors of Israel, shall be united with Israel in worship of the Lord, and shall share with Israel in the covenant mission of being a blessing in the midst of the earth (see covenant of blessing with Abraham). Egypt and Assyria would seem to be representative of all the Gentile nations. Especially significant are verse 21, "and the Egyptians will know the Lord in that day," and verse 25, "Blessed be Egypt my people, and Assyria the work of my hands, and Israel my heritage." There are indications in the text that some of this mission-ating was done by the Jews in gaining proselytes before the time of Christ; but the scope of the prophecy would seem to be wider than that. It has relevance as a text for a sermon on Christian missions. Change the names, and it applies to any nation today where "younger churches" are proving themselves a blessing in their witness unto the Lord of hosts, the God of Abraham, who is the God and Father of our Lord Jesus Christ.

Basic religious teachings of the text:

1. The witness unto the Lord in the land of Egypt, suggestive of a worldwide witness.

2. A saviour sent unto the oppressed in Egypt, suggestive of a world-wide salvation.

3. The Egyptians shall know the Lord, suggestive of a worldwide knowledge of God (see Isaiah 11:9).

4. The Egyptians also shall experience the "healing" of the Lord, suggestive of a worldwide spiritual ministry of healing.

5. Ancient enmities between Egypt, Assyria, and Israel, shall cease, suggestive of a worldwide brotherhood and a worldwide peace.

6. Israel shall be the third with Egypt and with Assyria, a blessing in the midst of the earth; suggestive of a worldwide fulfilment of the covenant of blessing with Abraham in Christ.

New Testament echoes of the text:

1. The universality of the Old Testament covenant becomes in the New Testament the universality of the gospel.

2. Galatians 3:14 states clearly the truth seen also in Isaiah 19:19-25, that the "blessing of Abraham" was intended also for the Gentiles.

3. Paul's teaching in Ephesians 2:11-22 is essentially the same as that in Isaiah 19; both indicate the breaking down of walls of partition between Jews and Gentiles.

Fourth Day of Prayer

TOPIC FOR THE DAY: "Thanksgiving."

TEXT: Isaiah 12.

THEME: Give thanks to the Lord —I will give thanks to Thee, O Lord.

Relation of the text to the topic:

The very heading given this chapter in our English Bible, "A Song of Thanksgiving," indicates that it is a fitting text for Thanksgiving Day. It is appropriate that we give thanks to God for national as well as for personal blessings, and for temporal blessings as well as spiritual. Isaiah 12 is a song of thanksgiving for God's salvation. The reference to Zion and its inhabitant makes it clear that it has reference to the salvation of God's people Israel. That salvation may be understood as being partly temporal, a deliverance from earthly enemies and oppressors, and partly spiritual, a restoration to the full enjoyment of the spiritual privileges of covenant fellowship from which their sins had so often separated them. It should not be difficult to make *the application* to our own land, omitting neither the spiritual nor the temporal blessings with which God has so abundantly blessed us during our national history. On the one hand the text urges to give thanks to the Lord (vs. 4-6); on the other hand it lays the words of thanksgiving upon our lips, "I will give thanks" (vs. 1-3).

Basic religious teachings of the text:

1. We should remember to give thanks for the blessings of God's salvation always.

2. Thanksgiving and trust in the Lord are closely linked in the Christian experience.

3. Thanksgiving leads to singing for joy of heart and thankfulness of spirit.

4. Thanksgiving leads also to prayer and witnessing.

5. The greatest reason for thanksgiving on the part of a nation is if it can truly say that God dwells in the midst of it.

New Testament echoes of the text:

Songs like the Benedictus, the Magnificat, and the Nunc Dimittis use a terminology that shows them to be steeped in the spiritual faith and tradition of the prophets and of the psalms.

Topical Preaching from Isaiah

The primary purpose in the writing of this book has been to demonstrate how preaching from Isaiah can be fitted into the Lutheran pericope system, which if faithfully followed by the preacher will assure the people of instruction in "the whole counsel of God" (Acts 20:27).

The book of Isaiah lends itself equally well, however, to topical preaching. For example, George Adam Smith says of the first chapter of Isaiah, "It is a clear complete statement of the points which were at issue between the Lord and His own all the time Isaiah was the Lord's prophet." In his article on Isaiah in International Standard Bible Encyclopedia, George L. Robinson characterizes chapter one as "an introduction in which the prophet strikes the chief notes of his entire book: viz., thoughtlessness (vs. 2-9), formalism in worship (vs. 10-17), pardon (vs. 18-23), and judgment (vs. 24-31)." These are certainly major notes in the message of Isaiah; but careful analysis of that message will add many more to the list.

A partial list of religiously relevant topics and appropriate texts follows. The discussion of each is necessarily limited; the primary purpose is careful and helpful selection of topics and texts.

1. The Holiness of God

A sermon could readily be preached on the characteristic Isaianic name for God, "The Holy One of Israel." It is found twenty-five times in the book of Isaiah and only five times elsewhere in the Old Testament. The first reference is in Isaiah 1:4 and the last in chapter 60:14.

An outstanding text is the so-called "Trisagion" in Isaiah 6:3. Equally majestic is the description of God in Isaiah 57:15. Significant also is the reference to "his holy spirit" (Hebrew, "the Spirit of his holiness") in Isaiah 63:10, 11.

In Biblical usage the concept of God's holiness includes both His transcendence and His "awful purity" (see Faber's hymn, "My God, how wonderful Thou art!"). Because God is holy it behooves man to walk humbly before Him (see Micah 6:8), and sin against Him is seen as rooted in pride. The frequent parallelism between "the Holy One of Israel" and "your Redeemer," as well as the significant declaration in ch. 57:15 that He whose name is Holy dwells with him who is of a contrite and humble spirit, makes it clear that God's holiness is related not only to His wrath and judgment, but also to His grace and salvation. A thorough word-study of the Hebrew word qodesh (holiness) would be helpful to the preacher at this point. The concept of God's holiness needs to be stressed in preaching today.

2. Sin

The Hebrew language uses a great many descriptive words for sin. Three of these are found in combination in Isaiah 59:12, as they are also in Psalm 32:1-2 and 51:1-2. The first is the Hebrew *pesha,* which means rebellion and transgression. The second is *hata'ath,* which means to miss the mark, the way, or the goal; or sin seen as failure and short-coming. The third is *awon,* one of several words translated *iniquity,* but with the more specific meaning of distortion, perversion, or crookedness. All three are found elsewhere in the book of Isaiah than in ch. 59:12.

Chapter 1:2-4 emphasizes the aspect of rebellion in Israel's sin (see also ch. 30:1, 9, and ch. 65:2). Their sin is described in ch. 1:4; described and confessed in ch. 59:1-15; and described and condemned in ch. 5:8-

23. In the description can be seen both the spiritual sin of apostasy from God and social sins of transgression against men. The sin of pride is always in the picture, and so is the lack of faith in the Lord. Sins of injustice and oppression are denounced frequently (see ch. 5:7; 3:14-15; 30:12; and 59:13). There is biting irony in the indictment of idolatry (ch. 44:12-17) and a touch of ridicule in the realistic description of drunkenness in ch. 28:7-8.

The list of sins in ch. 1:21-23 is only an index to the longer list contained in the book as a whole. A series of sermons could easily be preached on the theme of sin in the book of Isaiah, which in this respect is as modern as today's newspaper.

3. Repentance

The usual prophetic plea for repentance on the part of God's sinning people finds clear expression in the book of Isaiah. The best known passage is Isaiah 55:6-7. Even more urgent in tone is the plea in ch. 31: 6. Chapter 1:16-17 resembles the preaching of John the Baptist in calling for the fruits that befit repentance. The 13th verse of chapter 26 gives expression to an attitude of genuine repentance. So do verses 12-15a of chapter 59, for such a confession of national wickedness must come from a penitent heart. The theme of repentance is like a river channel that runs deep and wide through the prophetic preaching. In looking for appropriate texts we should not forget what Paul says in Romans 2:4, "Do you not know that God's kindness is meant to lead you to repentance?"

4. Forgiveness

The truth taught in Exodus 34:6-7, that the Lord is "a God merciful and gracious, slow to anger, and abounding in steadfast love and faithfulness, keeping steadfast love for thousands, forgiving iniquity and transgression and sin," is the teaching also of the book of Isaiah. The invitation to repentance in ch. 55:6-7 is coupled with the promise of mercy and pardon for him who repents. Isaiah himself had an experience of forgiveness and cleansing at the time of his call (see ch. 6:5-7). The most defensible interpretation of ch. 1:18 is the one which sees in it a summons to the experience of Divine pardon and cleansing from sin. The truth that God blots out transgressions and sins is dramatically affirmed in ch. 43:25, and is reaffirmed in ch. 44:22. It is a truth which is implied in the repeated reference to God as the Redeemer and Saviour of His people from the captivity which their sins had brought upon them; for Divine salvation even in this temporal sense had as its spiritual prerequisities repentance on the part of the people and remission of sins on the part of God.

5. Redemption

In frequent parallelism with "the Holy One of Israel" is the reference to God as "Redeemer." The concept is colored by the historical relationship between the Lord and His people Israel. Just as the Lord redeemed Israel out of the house of bondage in Egypt (see Exodus 20:2; Micah 6:4; Deuteronomy 7:8), so did He promise to redeem them from captivity in Babylon. But in each case the temporal deliverance had a spiritual accompaniment; for the deliverance was accomplished in accordance with the purpose and the terms of God's spiritual covenant with Israel. Oftentimes we see shining through the "times-coloring" of the redemption from the Babylonian Captivity the promise of a still greater and more spiritual redemption to come before the covenant reaches its consummation. There is in the redemption concept in the Old Testament a foreshadowing of the redemption that is in Christ Jesus (Romans 3:24) even when the direct reference is to a redemption experience nearer at hand and more limited in its spiritual implications. Recognizing both this real relationship and this actual difference between redemption as the prophets spoke of it and as the apostles preached it, we can readily see how an Old Testament text can be used for preaching the doctrine of redemption, not only from sin but from all manner of evil. It is not altogether a matter of direct prediction, though that is certainly not excluded from the prophetic preaching; but it is also a matter of continuing theological principle which is seen in different ways at different stages in God's redemptive activity.

Wilhelm Möller in his "Inledning till Gamla Testamentet" (translated from the German) gives an excellent outline of Isaiah 40-66 from Bracker's "Der Knecht Jahves" which sheds light on this concept of redemption. The outline is as follows:

A. Chs. 40-48. Cyrus, or the Jews' redemption from Babylon as a shadow (Swedish "skuggbild") of humanity's redemption from sin.

B. Chs. 49-57. Christ, or humanity's redemption from sin through the servant of the Lord.

C. Chs. 58-66. The new world, or the world's redemption from that which is transitory and passing away (Swedish "förgängelse") as a result of redemption from sin.

With this interpretative background it should not be difficult to preach redemption in its correct historical and spiritual sense from texts taken from the book of Isaiah. Among such texts may be listed ch. 50:2; 29:22; 35:8-9; 44:21-23; 51:10-11; 52:3, 9; 62:12; 63:9. In each case a wider context should be included in preparation if not in preaching.

6. Salvation

What has been said about redemption applies also to the concept of God's salvation. In the book of Isaiah as in the Old Testament generally it has a temporal as well as a spiritual aspect; but when we see the salvation in terms of God's covenant relationship with Israel, the spiritual aspect is the more significant of the two. When Isaiah says, "God is my salvation" (ch. 12:2), or proclaims to the Old Testament Zion "Your salvation comes" (ch. 62:11), or calls God "a just God and a Saviour" (ch. 45:21), and declares that there is no other God and no other Saviour (ch. 45:21-22 and 43:11), he confesses the same eternal truth which found its clearest and fullest expression when God sent His Son Jesus Christ into the world to be the Saviour of the world. There are many facets to the salvation of God, especially from the historical point of view, but it is nevertheless essentially one salvation; even as there is only one Saviour, though the Old Testament speaks of God (Jehovah) as that Saviour, and the New Testament usually speaks of the Saviour as being Jesus Christ.

One of the finest "salvation" texts in the book of Isaiah is ch. 45:20-

23. Another excellent text for a "salvation" sermon is ch. 30:15. Chapter 49:6 links salvation with the mission and ministry of the servant of the Lord. There are many promises of salvation to Israel as the covenant people of God, but just as many that seem to imply a salvation that is both everlasting and universal. There is no narrow provincialism in Isaiah's theology or in his soteriology. His message compares favorably in dimension with the New Testament gospel.

7. The Remnant

The doctrine of the remnant may seem to have a purely historical rather than a spiritual relevancy for the Bible reader today. It is true that it is a religious concept which belongs in a special sense to the history of the people of Israel. According to Isaiah 1:9 there was a remnant that was saved from conquest and destruction in the Assyrian invasion under Sennacherib (see also ch. 37:30-32). Isaiah 6:13 resembles Ezekiel 6:8 in that it indicates a remnant that should escape death in the day of conquest, captivity, and dispersion, such as the Babylonian Captivity; it refers to the remnant that went into the exile. But a far larger number of passages refer to a remnant that should return from the exile, and through whom God's original covenant purpose with Israel should be carried forward to its consummation.

There is religious relevancy in the recognition of the grace and power of God in relation to this remnant, just as there is in Jesus' words in Luke 12:32 with reference to the little flock, "Fear not, little flock, for it is your Father's good pleasure to give you the kingdom." There is religious relevancy also in the frequent emphasis on Divine chastening and on spiritual cleansing or purging in relation to the remnant (see Isaiah 4:3-4). The remnant concept does not refer only to the deliverance of a national group out of the hands of its enemies; it is essentially a spiritual concept involving a spiritual return to the Lord, the covenant God, in faith and obedience (see ch. 10:20-23). Without minimizing its historical reference to Israel it does seem legitimate to apply many of the truths connected with the remnant doctrine to the spiritual little flock of the New Testament. That is especially true of the beautiful "Fear not" passages in chs. 41:8-10, 13-14; 43:1, 5; 44:1-2, 8; and 54:4-8. It is also true of the "comfort" passages in chs. 12:1; 40:1-2; 49:13;

51:3, 12; 52:9; 61:2; 66:13. It was a part of the mission of the Messiah to banish all fear and to comfort all who mourn with the full assurance of God's salvation.

8. The Messiah

The clear and direct references to the Messiah are not many even in the book of Isaiah. Usually even when the viewpoint is eschatological it is the Lord (Jehovah) who is represented as active in redemption and salvation rather than one sent of God to be His representative or servant. The language is predominantly that of theology (the doctrine of God) rather than that of Christology (the doctrine of Christ). It is only in the light of the Incarnation that we see the deep Christological or Messianic implications even in the theology of the prophets. The salvation of God is accomplished by Christ.

Among the clear and direct predictions of the Messiah in the book of Isaiah are the following: the child Immanuel (7:14); the child who is to be the Prince of Peace (9:6); the root of Jesse (11: 1 ff.); the servant of the Lord who is to be for a covenant to the people and for a light to the nations (42:1-7 and 49:1-7); the suffering servant of the Lord (52:13-53:12; see also 50:4-9); and the one anointed with the Spirit of the Lord to preach good tidings of redemption and release (61:1-3). There are other prophecies which speak of the Messianic age without mention of the person of the Messiah. A good example is chapter 2:2-4. It is difficult to say whether "the branch of the Lord" in ch. 4:2-6 is a personal reference to the Messiah or not. It is a prophecy that deals with the Messianic age.

9. Faith and Hope

Isaiah 7:9b is a good text on the necessity and importance of faith (in the sense of trust) in God. See also ch. 43:10. Actually the word *trust* is used more often than the word *believe* in the Old Testament, and that is true also in Isaiah. The word *faith* does not occur at all; but that should not hinder us from recognizing the presence of the concept of faith in different language. Chapter 30:15 is a good description of the way faith acts, in quietness and confidence. Chapter 26:1-4 shows us the fruit of faith which is peace. An exhortation to trust in the Lord is found in ch. 26:4, and a confession of faith or trust in God as "my salvation" in ch. 12:2. There is a significant question in ch. 50:10 that makes a good sermon text: "Who among you fears the Lord and obeys the voice of his servant, who walks in darkness and has no light, yet trusts in the name of the Lord and relies upon his God?" The word *hope* is almost as infrequent as faith, but here also the concept is often present though the word is not used. It is used with real religious significance in ch. 51:5.

10. Love

There are two Old Testament words that can be translated as *love*. One is so translated in both AV and ASV, the Hebrew word *ahavah*. It is found in Isaiah 63:9, which makes an excellent text for a sermon on the love of God as illustrated in His love for His people Israel. The related verb from the same Hebrew root is found in Isaiah 61:8: God is said to love justice and to hate robbery and wrong. The verb also occurs in ch. 56:6 with reference to the love of God's servants for the name of the Lord. The ASV translation of Isaiah 38:17 makes a beautiful sermon text, but it is not a faithful translation of the Hebrew where the word for love does not occur. Another good text on love is ch. 43:4, where God says of His people, "Because you are precious in my eyes, and honored, and I love you, I give men in return for you, peoples in exchange for your life."

The second Old Testament word meaning love is the Hebrew *hesed,* which is one of the most significant words in Biblical theology. It has been variously translated in AV and ASV as lovingkindness, mercy, kindness, and goodness. The translation in RSV as *stedfast love* is excellent; for the Hebrew *hesed* stands for *faithfulness* to a covenant of *love.* The word is not used as often by Isaiah as by some other Old Testament writers, but Isaiah 54:8, 10, and Isaiah 63:7 are two good texts on God's steadfast love. The word occurs also in ch. 16:5, a verse with Messianic implications through its reference to the covenant with David. The same is true in ch. 55:3 where it is used in the plural, which RSV interprets as "my stedfast, sure love for David."

11. Righteousness

Righteousness is a major concept in the book of Isaiah as it is in all the prophets. The following are a few illustrative texts:

1. Ch. 5:7. God looked in vain for righteousness from Israel as the fruit desired from His vineyard.

2. Ch. 5:16. The Holy God shows Himself holy in righteousness.

3. Ch. 11:4, 5. Righteousness is an attribute of the Messiah as well as of God. (See also ch. 16:5.)

4. Ch. 26:9-10. Righteousness is learned from God's judgments in the earth.

5. Ch. 32:16-17. The effect of righteousness will be peace. (See ch. 57:21, "There is no peace, says my God, for the wicked.")

6. Ch. 33:5. God will fill Zion with justice and righteousness.

7. Ch. 45:19. "I the Lord speak the truth, I declare what is right."

8. Ch. 59:9, 14. The confession that righteousness stands afar off.

9. Ch. 64:6. Another confession, that "all our righteous deeds are like a polluted garment."

To these should be added the reference to *justice* (Hebrew mishpat). The parallelism with righteousness in Isaiah 5:7 and elsewhere suggests that justice is one form in which righteousness is expressed. According to Micah 6:8 it is one of three major requirements of God which He has made known to man as His good and gracious will for human life. The statement in ch. 59:15b with reference to the condition of national wickedness is still true: "The Lord saw it, and it displeased him that there was no justice." "Seek justice" (ch. 1:17) is a major note in the preaching of the prophets.

12. Peace

Peace is just as prominent a concept in the book of Isaiah as righteousness and the two are often closely associated. Among the following illustrations are some excellent sermon texts:

1. Ch. 2:4. "In the latter days" they shall neither learn nor wage war any more.

2. Ch. 9:6-7. The Messiah is called preeminently the Prince of Peace, and his government is said to be marked by righteousness, justice, and peace.

3. Ch. 11:6-9. A prophecy of a future peace like that in the original Paradise.

4. Ch. 26:3. Trust in the Lord leads to perfect peace.

5. Ch. 26:12. The Lord will ordain peace for His people.

6. Ch. 32:17. The effect of righteousness will be peace.

7. Ch. 39:8. The wistful hope of Hezekiah, "There will be peace and security in my days."

8. Ch. 48:18. In the way of obedience to God's commandments there is righteousness and peace.

9. Ch. 48:22. "There is no peace," says the Lord, "for the wicked." See also ch. 57:21.

10. Ch. 52:7. The tidings of peace and salvation are good tidings.

11. Ch. 53:5 (ASV). The chastisement of our peace was upon him, the suffering servant of the Lord.

12. Ch. 54:10. My covenant of peace shall not be removed, says the Lord.

13. Ch. 55:12. God's people shall be led forth in peace.

14. Ch. 57:2. The upright man enters into peace when he dies.

15. Ch. 59:8. The national confession of sins includes the confession that "the way of peace they know not."

13. Faithfulness and Truth

The words *faithfulness* and *truth* both come from the same Hebrew root. Starting with the verb, Amen, which in its simplest form means to *be firm,* we find several derivatives, all of them embodying the basic idea of something that is firm, and therefore trustworthy and dependable. It is the causative form of the verb that is translated *believe.* One noun is *'emeth,* which is quite regularly translated as *truth* but sometimes as *faithfulness;* for the essential element in the Hebrew concept of truth is that which is faithful and true, i.e., dependable. Another noun, *'emunah,* is regularly translated as *faithfulness,* though in Habakkuk 2:4 it is this word which is rendered *faith.* We can see how closely related the concept involved in these words is to that of *hesed.* It is significant that *hesed* and *'emeth* often occur in poetic parallelism, as in Exodus 34:6 and frequently in the Psalms. And yet there is a distinction between the two, in that *hesed* is associated more with God's covenant love which is a steadfast love and *'emeth* is associated more with His covenant promises which are truth, i.e., faithful and true and dependable. Both words, however, extend into the area of life and conduct as a whole. In Isaiah 1:21 "the faithful city" is seen in contrast with the symbol of the harlot. The witnesses in ch. 8:2 could be called either "reliable" (RSV) or "faithful" (ASV). Faithfulness as well as righteousness is a part of the spiritual and moral equipment of the Messiah (ch. 11:5; see also 16:5). In Ch. 49:7 the fulfilment of the prophecy seems to be guaranteed by "the Lord, who is faithful." The wonderful things that God has done are seen to be in fulfilment of "plans formed of old, faithful and sure" (ch. 25:1). "The God of truth" in ch. 65:16 is literally "the God of Amen" (significant in the light of Luther's explanation of the word Amen in relation to prayer). As used in Isaiah 10:20 and 48:1 the phrase "in truth" is equivalent to "in sincerity." In ch. 59:14-15 the lack of truth seems to mean the lack of honesty and fidelity. Especially significant as a text is Isaiah 45:19, "I the Lord speak the truth, I declare what is right." The close connection between faith and faithfulness is seen in ch. 26:2, where "keeps faith" means "is faithful."

14. Knowledge of God

When the prophets speak of *knowing God* they mean an experiential knowledge. A true knowledge of God leads to faith in God and also to right action in relation to His commandments (see Jeremiah 22:16). The mighty acts of God, as in the days of the Exodus-redemption, are designed to teach men the true knowledge of God. There are frequent references in the book of Isaiah to this knowledge of God and also to the lack of it. The forward look of prophecy is to the day when "the earth shall be full of the knowledge of the Lord as the waters cover the sea" (Isaiah 11:9; Habakkuk 2:14; Jeremiah 31:34).

Among other significant texts are these:

1. Ch. 1:3. The indictment, "Israel does not know, my people do not understand," enlarges upon the statement in verse 2 concerning the

rebellion of the children that God had reared and brought up.

2. Ch. 5:13. "My people go into exile for want of knowledge."

3. Ch. 19:21. A prediction that the Lord will make Himself known to the Egyptians, and that the Egyptians will know the Lord.

4. Ch. 41:20. The purpose with God's redemptive activity and with His blessings upon His redeemed people is "that men may see and know, may consider and understand together, that the hand of the Lord has done this, the Holy One of Israel has created it."

5. Ch. 43:10-11. "You are my witnesses," says the Lord, "and my servant whom I have chosen, that you may know and believe me and understand that I am He."

6. Ch. 45:3-6. In commissioning Cyrus to deliver Israel God's purpose is that both Cyrus and Israel and men everywhere may know that there is no other God and Saviour than the Lord God of Israel.

7. Ch. 49:23. The statement, "Then you will know that I am the Lord," is reminiscent of the Exodus and of the book of Ezekiel.

8. Ch. 49:26. The prediction, "Then all flesh shall know that I am the Lord your Saviour, and your Redeemer."

9. Ch. 50:4, 7. The servant says, "I know that I shall not be put to shame."

10. Ch. 52:6. The introduction to this verse is found in vs. 3: when the Lord redeems His people they learn to know His name.

11. Ch. 58:2. An ironic reference to a people that thinks it knows the ways of God but does not.

12. Ch. 59:8. Israel does not know the way of peace.

13. Ch. 59:12. The confession of the prophet in behalf of his people, "we know our iniquities."

14. Ch. 60:16. The language resembles that of ch. 49:26, but here it is addressed to Israel as God's people: "and you shall know that I, the Lord, am your Saviour and your Redeemer, the Mighty One of Jacob."

One thing should be evident from even a cursory reading of these passages: to know the Lord means more than an intellectual knowledge, or simply to know about Him. A true knowledge of God is much more closely related to faith and assurance, and to a life in harmony with our faith. It is a dynamic concept wherever it is found in the Old Testament. True knowledge of God leads to right action in faith and obedience.

15. Obedience

The emphasis on obedience is much more frequent in Jeremiah than it is in Isaiah. It is often implied in Isaiah as the reverse side of the indictment for rebellion (see ch. 1:2-4). A very good sermon text on the theme of obedience is Isaiah 1:19-20. Another excellent text is ch. 48:18, which we have listed previously under both righteousness and peace. As a "disciple," or as one who is taught, the servant of the Lord sets an example of obedience in the face of suffering and shame (ch. 50: 4-6). Chapter 42:24 is an indictment of Israel because they would not walk in the ways of the Lord nor obey His law. We can see in the background the covenant as set forth in Exodus 19:5-6. "If you will obey my voice and keep my covenant, you shall be my own possession among all peoples; for all the earth is mine, and you shall be to me a kingdom of priests and a holy nation."

16. A Humble Spirit

The classic text on this theme is Isaiah 57:15. (See also under the Holiness of God.) The word *humble* is not used in ch. 66:2, but the thought is expressed by the related words *poor* and *contrite*. The humble spirit is the opposite of the spirit of pride and of self-sufficiency and of rebellion. It is a spirit that is closely related to penitence and faith. One of the three major Divine requirements as listed in Micah 6:8 is "to walk humbly with your God."

17. The Fear of the Lord

A good text is found in Isaiah 33:6, especially the last line, "the fear of the Lord is his treasure." For a discussion of the pronoun before "treasure," see First Sunday after Trinity. In Isaiah 11:2 the fear of the Lord is one of the gifts of the Spirit with which the Messiah is said to be endowed; and according to vs. 3 of the same chapter "his delight shall be in the fear of the Lord." In ch. 50:10 the concept of the fear of the Lord is united with that of faith and of obedience in one striking and significant text.

18. Spiritual and Ethical Sincerity in Worship

This frequent, urgent note in prophetic preaching is found especially in Isaiah 1:10-17 and 66:1-4. It is vividly summed up in George Adam Smith's translation of the last clause in ch. 1:13: "I cannot away with wickedness and worship." It indicates sharply the Divine disapproval of formalism in worship. It contrasts just as sharply with the Divine approval of a humble and a contrite spirit (see ch. 57:15). Such a spirit of humble contrition will lead to a truly spiritual worship, and to an earnest concern about ethical righteousness of life. A vivid picture of hypocracy in worship is found in ch. 29:13. This people professed to have a fear of the Lord but it didn't come from the heart: it was only "a commandment of men learned by rote." With such worship God is not pleased. Neither is He pleased when men think that they can divorce the religion of the sanctuary from the religion of life.

19. God in History

Isaiah 10:5-27 is a good text for presenting God's place and purpose in human history, in relation to the great nations such as Assyria in the prophet's day or its counterpart in our own, and in relation to the spiritual remnant of Israel that represents the kingdom of God. With reference to this theme, see Scherer's "Event in Eternity" (PP. 11-12). Other chapters that reveal to us Isaiah the statesman, with a counsel that reflects God's purpose in definite historical situations, are these: ch. 7, with reference to Ahaz and the Syrian situation; chs. 8, 10, with reference to the Assyrian situation; chs. 30, 31, with reference to a proposed Egyptian alliance; chs. 36-37, with reference to the invasion of Sennacherib in the days of Hezekiah; ch. 39, with reference to the messengers from Merodachbaladan and the coming Babylonian situation; and chs. 40-48, with reference to the coming deliverance from Babylon through Cyrus, who is called the Lord's anointed (ch. 45:1).

20. The Incomparable Greatness of God

It is especially chapter 40 that gives us a picture of the living God, the Almighty Creator of heaven and earth, who is also sovereign in history. Good preaching texts on this theme of God's greatness and power abound in the chapter. One verse that stands out above the others is vs. 28. In chapter 44 the contrast between the helpless idols and the living God is vividly set forth. Throughout the latter part of the book of Isaiah this greatness of God is seen in two ways: it can be seen in that He alone is able to predict events before they come to pass, and does so predict through His servants the prophets; it can be seen also in His power to perform, or to bring to pass that which He predicts, and especially that which He promises in the way of redemption and release for His people.

21. God's Wisdom in Counsel

The parable from husbandry in Isaiah 28:23-29 is interpreted in verse 29: "This also comes from the Lord of hosts; he is wonderful in counsel, and excellent in wisdom." Wisdom and counsel are also associated with the Messiah in ch. 11:2. In ch. 9:6 "Wonderful Counsellor" is one of the names given to the Messiah.

22. The Day of the Lord

The two chief references to the day of the Lord are in Isaiah 2:12 ff. and in 13:6 ff. From the description given here and elsewhere in the prophets it can be seen to be a day of judgment. The passage in Isaiah 13-14 has reference to Babylon. In chapter two the judgment seems to begin with God's own people Israel but includes "all that is proud and lofty among men." The prediction or the pronouncement of judgment is a frequent note in the message of Isaiah and is not limited to the concept of the day of the Lord. A significant text is ch. 3:13-15, where the prophet declares: "The Lord enters into judgment with the elders and princes of his people." In the Messianic prophecy in ch. 4:2-6 the cleansing of Zion that leads to a holy remnant is said to be accomplished "by a spirit of judgment and by a spirit of burning." Judgment may have other purposes than to punish and to destroy; it may be a means of cleansing and chastening, leading to repentance and righteousness and restored covenant fellowship. See Isaiah 26:8-10. While it is still the day of grace here on earth God's judgments are closely linked in loving purpose with His redemption.

23. The Light of the Lord

The concept of God as light, or the concept of a Divine light shining into the darkness in which men are represented as walking, is frequent in the book of Isaiah. The nature of the darkness varies: sometimes it seems to be predominantly spiritual in character, at other times it seems to signify temporal adversity or calamity that has overtaken the nation of Israel. God as the light suggests salvation as well as revelation.

1. Ch. 2:5. The invitation to the house of Jacob, "Come, let us walk in the light of the Lord."
2. Ch. 9:2. The prediction, "The people who walked in darkness have seen a great light; those who dwelt in a land of deep darkness, on them has light shined." A Messianically significant prophecy.
3. Ch. 10:17. "The light of Israel" stands in poetic parallelism with "his Holy One." The light is here associated with fire as a symbol of judgment. God is a consuming fire (Hebrews 12:29; Isaiah 33:14).
4. Ch. 42:6 and 49:6. The servant of the Lord is given as a light to the nations.
5. Ch. 51:4. The prediction that God's justice will go forth for a light to the peoples. The context is that of God's righteous salvation of His people.
6. Ch. 58:8. "Your light" stands in parallelism with "your healing," and both seem to refer to an experience of God's gracious presence in a renewal of His original covenant with them to be their God. It is here made contingent upon a right seeking of the Lord (see vs. 9-10).
7. Ch. 60:1-3. The exhortation to God's people who are about to experience God's salvation, "Arise, shine; for your light has come, and the glory of the Lord has risen upon you." A Messianic prophecy.
8. Ch. 60:19-20. In the day of final fulfilment of God's covenant and of the glorification of God's Zion there shall be no further need of sun

or moon to give light; for "the Lord will be your everlasting light, and your God will be your glory." The language is very similar to that of the book of Revelation.

24. The Glory of God

The concept of God's glory is closely related to the concept of God as light. In Isaiah 60:19 God is said to be both the light and the glory of His people. God's glory is also closely related to His holiness. Delitzsch refers to God's glory as "His manifested holiness." The holiness of God cannot be seen; it can only be apprehended as a truth. For God's holiness signifies His essential Deity, His transcendence, His spotless purity, His separation from men as the One who is "altogether other." As the Holy One He is "invisible" (Hebrews 11:27). But the Holy One can manifest Himself and His presence to men in ways which can be seen. This manifestation of God is closely associated with the concept of His glory. It may be manifested *to* His people, so that they see it; it may be manifested *upon* His people, so that they share it. When experienced by His people it leads to the giving of glory to God, in the sense of praise.

A few significant illustrations from the book of Isaiah:

1. Ch. 2:10, 19. The glory of His majesty as seen in His judgment power.

2. Ch. 4:5. A symbolic portrayal of the glory of God's people after they have been cleansed from their sin and have become again "a holy nation" according to the terms of the covenant with them (see Exodus 19:6).

3. Ch. 6:3. The Trisagion: "Holy, holy, holy is the Lord of hosts; the whole earth is full of His glory."

4. Ch. 28:5. The prediction that "in that day the Lord of hosts will be a crown of glory, and a diadem of beauty, to the remnant of His people."

5. Ch. 35:2. Another prediction, of the day when "they shall see the glory of the Lord, the majesty of our God."

6. Ch. 40:5. A prediction like the one above: "and the glory of the Lord shall be revealed, and all flesh shall see it together." See Luke 3:3-6.

7. Ch. 42:8. The declaration of God, "I am the Lord, that is my name; my glory I give to no other, nor my praise to graven images."

Here *my glory* means the *praise* that is due me. See vs. 12: "Let them give glory to the Lord, and declare His praise in the coastlands."

8. Ch. 59:19. "The name of the Lord" and "his glory" stand together in parallelism. Both signify a manifestation of God.

9. Ch. 60:2. A promise to God's people that "the Lord will arise upon you, and His glory will be seen upon you." In vs. 1, and again in vs. 19, light and glory seem to be synonymous.

10. Ch. 66:18, 19. The promise that a time is coming when nations "that have not heard my fame or seen my glory" "shall come and shall see my glory" "and they shall declare my glory among the nations."

25. New Heavens and a New Earth

The direct references are in Isaiah 65:17 and 66:22, but the verses should be studied in context. The "new things" spoken of in ch. 42:9; 43:19; and 48:6 may have some relationship to this new heaven and new earth. The outlook is eschatological in all five passages. There are many other passages in Isaiah with an eschatological outlook that is strikingly similar to that in the book of Revelation. It can be seen especially in chapters 24-27 and in chapters 58-66, the section to which Bracker gave the title, "The new world, or the world's redemption from that which is transitory and passing away." The covenant hope shines brightly in the book of Isaiah. There will come a day of complete and final redemption. There will come a day when the earth shall be full of the knowledge of the Lord as the waters cover the sea. There will come a day when nation shall not lift up sword against nation, neither shall they learn war any more. There will come a day when the Lord God will swallow up death forever and will wipe away tears from all faces. There will come a day when the Lord God creates new heavens and a new earth in which righteousness dwells. There will come a day when the kingdom shall be the Lord's. Through the haze of the "times-coloring" that so often seems to cloud the picture, we can see the goal in glory shining from afar. And we do not need to see every step in the way in order to keep our eyes on that goal!

Great Texts in the Book of Isaiah

At the risk of what may seem to be needless repetition we shall conclude this "preacher's approach" to the book of Isaiah by listing in their order of appearance some of the great texts in the book and the reason for calling them so. These are texts that enunciate principles or truths on which the preacher could preach effectively without knowing a thing about the historical situation to which they were first addressed. There are such texts in Isaiah. A little knowledge of the historical situation will often help to clothe them with the vivid concreteness of life; but they do speak a clear message regardless of background because they represent either eternal principles of truth or oft-repeated human situations to which the truth is addressed. We shall try to make the list a truly selective one. It is the privilege of every preacher to add to it from his own reading of the book of Isaiah.

1. Ch. 1:2-3. God speaks as a loving Father of children who have rebelled against His love, not knowing what is good for them.

2. Ch. 1:13. God cannot endure the combination of wickedness and worship, or a religion divorced from ethics.

3. Ch. 1:18. A gracious invitation of God to reason together until it becomes clear to us that sin needs to be forgiven and that God does forgive sin.

4. Ch. 2:5. Another invitation, extended by the prophet, to walk in the light of the Lord, or in the light of His revealed will and truth.

5. Ch. 3:15. An appeal to the conscience of those who are guilty of oppressing the helpless poor.

6. Ch. 5:7. The tragic truth that God often looks for the fruit of righteousness from His people and does not find it.

7. Ch. 7:9b. The imperative need of faith in the life of men and of nations if they shall be established in their ways.

8. Ch. 8:20. There is no other place to find the light of life than in the teaching and the testimony of God's Word.

9. Ch. 9:6. The gift by God of a child who is the Prince of Peace is still mankind's only real hope of peace.

10. Ch. 10:15. Why should any man or nation foolishly forget that their power is not their own but is given by God with a purpose, for a season?

11. Ch. 11:9. The promise of a day when all men shall know the Lord gives hope also of peace on earth.

12. Ch. 12:2. An ever relevant confession of faith in God as my salvation, my strength, and my song.

13. Ch. 24:16a. Songs of praise, coming from the ends of the earth, give glory to God as the Righteous One (see Jesus, the Holy and Righteous One, Acts 3:14).

14. Ch. 25:1. I will praise God because He faithfully performs what He has planned and promised.

15. Ch. 25:8. God's word gives His people the sure hope of victory over death and of freedom from sorrow.

16. Ch. 26:3. The mind that is stayed on God in faithful trust is kept by Him in perfect peace.

17. Ch. 26:9b-10. God sends judgments on earth in order to teach men the lesson of righteousness.

18. Ch. 26:13. This is the confession of those who have turned from serving other lords to acknowledge God alone as Lord!

19. Ch. 29:13-14. God wants a religion of the heart and not only of the lips.

20. Ch. 29:15-16. God's Woe is upon those who think they can ignore God as if He did not see and had no power to act.

21. Ch. 30:15. God's way of salvation is the way of quiet, confident faith in Him.

22. Ch. 30:18. The Lord waits to be gracious and merciful to all those who wait for Him. He is ready when we are ready.

23. Ch. 30:21. When our ears are open to hear God's word He will direct us in the way in which we are to walk.

24. Ch. 31:6. A plea to men in every generation who have "deeply revolted" against God: Turn back to Him!

25. Ch. 32:16-17. Righteousness results in peace, therefore we must seek righteousness *first* (Matthew 6:33).

26. Ch. 33:2. A good morning prayer, and a good prayer when troubles come our way!

27. Ch. 40:1-2. God be praised that I too am commanded to *comfort* God's people with the assurance of the forgiveness of sins!

28. Ch. 40:10-11. "God of mercy, God of might,
In love and pity infinite!"

29. Ch. 40:28-31. The Lord, the living God, the eternal Creator, does not faint, and to them who do faint He gives power and increases strength: a promise for young and old!

30. Ch. 41:13. It isn't so difficult not to be afraid when we have a God who holds us by the hand and promises to help us!

31. Ch. 43:10-13. We are witnesses to what God has done, and we know and believe that there is no other Saviour.

32. Ch. 43:25. A word to remember when we begin to speak and act as if we thought that God needed to be persuaded to forgive sins by some act of ours. It is His Nature to forgive if we only let Him!

33. Ch. 48:17-18. The way of obedience to God's commands is a good way wherein is experienced righteousness and peace like a river (see Deuteronomy 5:29).

34. Ch. 49:14-16. God does not forget His people! A word for Israel, a word also for us as Christians.

35. Ch. 50:10. Can I, can you, say in answer to this question that our faith is like this?

36. Ch. 51:12-13. A good question for a generation that trembles with fear before the fury of the Hitlers and the Mussolinis and the Stalins and forgets the Lord.

37. Ch. 53:4-6. It was for me!

38. Ch. 54:8. God's chastening is for a moment, His love and compassion are everlasting.

39. Ch. 54:10. God's covenant is a covenant of steadfast love and of abiding peace.

40. Ch. 55:1-3. Man does not live by bread alone but by every word that proceeds from the mouth of God.

41. Ch. 55:6-9. An urgent invitation and a reassuring promise to sinners!

42. Ch. 56:7. God's house is a house of prayer for all peoples.

43. Ch. 57:15-16. The Holy God who inhabits eternity dwells also with each one of us who is of a contrite and humble spirit. My God, how wonderful Thou art!

44. Ch. 58:6-7. You cannot serve God acceptably unless you also serve your fellowman in his need.

45. Ch. 59:1-2. If God does not hear our prayers it is not because He cannot hear: there is unrepented sin that stands in the way!

184 PREACHING FROM ISAIAH

46. Ch. 59:12-15a. In the face of great national wickedness Christians should learn to confess that "we" have sinned.

47. Ch. 60:1-3. To whom the light of God has come comes also the command: Let your light shine!

48. Ch. 61:1. As a believer in him who speaks these words, the Christ, I too am called and sent to bring good tidings.

49. Ch. 62:6-7. It is the duty of the spiritual watchmen upon the walls of Zion to put God in remembrance of His promises; for He wants to be reminded of them in believing prayer.

50. Ch. 63:9. God is like that still in relation to us!

51. Ch. 65:24. In its fulness this promise belongs to the new heavens and the new earth, but even now the Christian discovers that it is often true.

52. Ch. 66:1-2. God is a Spirit, and they that worship Him must worship in spirit and truth.

Index of Texts